THE POWER OF STORY

BOOKS BY HAROLD R. JOHNSON

FICTION

Billy Tinker
Back Track
Charlie Muskrat
The Cast Stone
Corvus
The Björkan Sagas

NONFICTION

Two Families: Treaties and Government
Firewater: How Alcohol is Killing My People (and Yours)
Clifford
Peace and Good Order: The Case for Indigenous Justice in Canada
Cry Wolf

The Power of Story

*On Truth, the Trickster, and New Fictions
for a New Era*

Harold R. Johnson

Foreword by Tracey Lindberg

BIBLIOASIS

Windsor, Ontario

FIRST EDITION
10 9 8 7 6 5 4 3

Title: The power of story : on truth, the trickster, and new fictions for a new era / Harold R Johnson.
Names: Johnson, Harold, 1954-2022, author.
Identifiers: Canadiana (print) 20220256322 | Canadiana (ebook) 20220393168
    ISBN 9781771964876 (softcover) | ISBN 9781771964883 (ebook)
Subjects: LCSH: Storytelling. | LCSH: Storytelling—Social aspects. | LCSH: Rhetoric—Social aspects. | LCSH: Narration (Rhetoric)—Social aspects.
Classification: LCC P96.S78 J64 2022 | DDC 808.5/43—dc23

Edited and typeset by Vanessa Stauffer
Copyedited by Rachel Ironstone
Cover designed by Ingrid Paulson

Published with the generous assistance of the Canada Council for the Arts, which last year invested $153 million to bring the arts to Canadians throughout the country, and the financial support of the Government of Canada. Biblioasis also acknowledges the support of the Ontario Arts Council (OAC), an agency of the Government of Ontario, which last year funded 1,709 individual artists and 1,078 organizations in 204 communities across Ontario, for a total of $52.1 million, and the contribution of the Government of Ontario through the Ontario Book Publishing Tax Credit and Ontario Creates.

Harold passed away February 9, 2022, a couple of weeks after completing the substantive edits for this book. My husband was a brilliant man and gifted storyteller. His last words are powerful and are dedicated to all peoples. He encourages us to think about where we came from and the future we choose. We have the ability to change our story.

JOAN JOHNSON, June 2022

Sometime in the last few years, Harold asked me if I would review one of his manuscript drafts. We were open and honest with each other—Harold, because he was with everyone. Me, because I was so with him. In my review of the draft, I found some language or logic troubling. In communicating my thoughts I drafted and re-drafted them and even considered not sending them. In the end, I communicated as we do: frankly, but in this instance worrying that I had overstepped a boundary or that he might react in a way which would change our relationship. He wrote back and was generous in his response, thanking me and acknowledging that writers' references are era specific and that someday he would be taken to task for his ideas and language aging out—but this was not that day. The pragmatism and elemental truth in that struck me and sits with me today as I read his last work.

Part of me wants to cherish it and treat it as precious. Part of me wants to read it as Harold would read our work: kindly critical + critically kind. There is a line early in *The Power of Story* where he writes about working too hard and not taking enough time: "I spent too much time working and not enough time with my family. In real terms I would have been much richer if I had not pursued economic wealth over mental, emotional, and spiritual wealth." It is not remorseful, but a kind gift. I want to text him. Call him or write him and let him know that he couldn't be *this* writer if he had not been so hard-working. But, he knew what he was saying and said what he meant. He wouldn't need me to soothe or caretake him.

He said what he meant. At the time that he wrote his work, it was Harold's truth. Having read his fiction, and seen the crossover between life and the living, in my experience as a lawyer, critic of law schools and the Canadian legal system, and creative thinker, I find myself nodding often with his work. Also, I find myself shaking my head and arguing with him—both prospects I think would make his eyes twinkle. Making us think and feel is a rich gift that I am thankful he left us, on and off the page.

When we were both youngish—I traveled to Cambridge to visit friends. They were having a writing group gathering on the night I visited them. Harold was there. We all read from our work and Harold told us what he was inspired by and reading. He was a true believer in the understanding that we could learn something from everyone. It wasn't the written word alone that he cherished; he loved people and their language, their silence, and their thoughtfulness. He could sit and enjoy your company or your silence because he was deeply engaged in experiencing, enjoying—living. In this work, Harold is fully engaged with the richness of living and life. In reading this, I am aware that time was running as he was writing—but he is as ever patient and involved with us not just as readers, but as fellow storytellers. There is such optimism and love in his logic—it thrums with the heartbeat of a writer who cares deeply about the stories we tell. He is not so egocentric as to be enchanted by his own voice. In this work, he opens the door to young, old, women, two-spirited peoples and all animate nations (winged, gilled, spectacular, natural) as housing the means to care for the planet, each other and our selves.

Part of his gift was normalizing fantastic. Being able to imagine made it possible to do and be. At one point in our careers we both lived in Saskatoon. We were both asked to read / perform for an audience at the

Broadway Theatre. Harold read from what I think was to become *Billy Tinker*. My memory is of a shy, quiet, confident voice coming from him. It was surprising in some measure, because he was so smartly engaged with critique and discussion of Canadian law and its potential (for harm and good) that hearing him as a fiction writer was a moment I remember. To have been able to work up north, led a camp life, toiled for the navy, gone to law school *and* be a creative writer seemed so nearly impossible. Nearly impossible, though, was the space from which he lovelaboured, I think. What seemed common trajectories: legal thinker writing a treatise on treaties (*Two Families: Treaties and Government*) and a creative writer publishing a work of fiction a year later (*Charlie Muskrat*) was rare enough. Later in his career, he would be called genre-bending (*Clifford*), border-crossing (*The Bjorkan Sagas*) and a creative philosopher (*Cry Wolf*) as his voice became strongly identifiable and home to crossover between stories as fact and truth and fiction. Award nominated and winning, Harold's later publications were celebrated because of the strength of his voice and the commitment to the accessibility of story. Both *Firewater* and *Peace and Good Order: The Case for Indigenous Justice in Canada* stand out because they are passionate, intellectually accessible, and stories that need to be told.

In this work (and I am having a hard time writing "final"), Harold emphasizes and expands upon the ideas he teased out most notably in *Firewater*: we are the stories we tell and we become the stories we tell ourselves. The occasion is a multi-cultural and multi-faith gathering at his and his partner Joan's home, where the dock sits on the spot where lake meets river. In this way, we are introduced to what is a really welcoming and warm narrative about the places held and created by story and the work and possible worlds of storytelling. Within it, he sees the gathering of people from different and differing backgrounds as "a chance for humanity"—and as a reader (almost as a listener) we are introduced into the scope and possibility of story that he gifts us.

Conversationally, Harold tells us of the violent removal of his people from the Prince Albert National Park when his mom was twelve years old and he reminds us that survival and survivance are not wholly dependent upon physical labour—but also upon our capacity to remember, create, and share stories. There is less dogma and more space devoted to creation and creatively developing, reframing and altering the stories that we tell. At the start and at the end he relies upon our smartest selves to interpret the stories he has written about Trickster / Older Brother, Wisahkicahk.

Grounding his time around the fire, weaving stories and braiding experience, potential truths, and possible worlds, he begins to lead listeners / readers through the beauty that stories can create and reveal and the devastation and destruction that stories can result in and perpetuate.

He leads us through areas fraught with colonial shadowy stories attached to and secured by ideologies of supremacy, superiority, and just enrichment. Through the lens of story we are able to understand how the violence of colonialism is upheld by self-serving and reifying narratives about tenure, private property, corporatization, economies, war, and sovereignty, and Harold reminds us that these are new(er) stories, the authority of which is embedded in and is used to enrich newcomers and cousins on Indigenous territories. He does not couch any of this discussion in terms of victimhood but he does address the continuing cost exacted by telling stories of rightfulness, righteousness, rights, and residency in a settler validating and valorizing voice.

Perhaps it is fitting that the stories which sustain and strengthen the work are those stories he shares about relationality. Indigenous and non-Indigenous relations solidified through treaty-making and the ensuing responsibilities to each other as family members. The teaching shared with respect to this relationality (to setters as cousins, to animal, plant, and other life). The complex interrelationships to all life that surrounds us, including "the standing nation of trees, the four-legged nations, the flying nations of birds, the swimming nations of fish, and the crawling nations of insects," necessitates both care and careful storytelling.

This includes care in not generalizing, aggregating, or stereotyping and some of his work and writing made me uncomfortable enough to stop, pause, re-read and return to sections. If I read and understand the work as it is written—without cynicism or rage—I am more able to envision the story as intended. Hopeful. Careful. Powerful. Some of the language (past tense verbs as related to governance, women's roles, authority, agency) requires us as readers to contest, contradict, or question what he has written. Other portions of the work are rich and require deep thinking, discussion, and dissemination. His stories related to ceremonies, children and Elders' independence, spiritual connectedness and storytelling as an act of love, within which we shower our characters with care and treat them respectfully, supports the fullest iteration of our lives and work as dear and loving. Story allows us our voice and perception.

For it is in his discussion of the definition and interpretation of story as applied to race, scientific discovery and advancement, and truth that Harold gifts us immeasurably in this work. Breaking down notions of absolutism and fundamentalism as tied to truth (which, he reminds us, does not exist in nature or otherwise) serves only to validate some means of creating "knowledge" without acknowledging that all things (science, theories, historical writings) are someone's version of a story—affixed to a goal of establishing belief as it validates privilege, wealth, inequality.

He steps beyond story as detailing to storytelling as a loving act. His loving act is well in evidence as he educates his audience about the storied richness of hope, love, and happiness. Discussing our possible futures, he leans into the story shared by knowledge keepers about our capacity as beings:

> Imagine love so immense that a mere human is incapable of enduring it all. Imagine happiness, likewise, so intense that at its height it is hard to endure. Then add to this the experience of being a spirit in a physical body, knowing that the only person in charge of your life is yourself. You are whole and complete. You are plugged in to the neural networks, the mycelia, the root systems of

the forest. You experience and can translate energy and frequencies. You are repeatedly told by the spirits of the plants and animals and insects, "you are a beautiful human being."

Vesting in the fantastic, he reminds us that we do have agency and autonomy, but that we also have spirit helpers to work with us. Women's agency and autonomy are rich and storied; humanity's capacity for goodness rich and unfettered. He imagines and stories a world where we can be hopeful and healing; where we can connect and share stories that emancipate and govern us collectively. In circles, in our visits, and in our families—we can write and tell our story in a unified voice. As family.

Ultimately, Harold Johnson envisions and shares a possible future where we relate our story as a family with shared responsibilities and love. This loving gift—this potential for familial love bigger than self and more caring than seems possible at times—is the best story and is perhaps his biggest of all the gifts he has given us.

TRACEY LINDBERG
W̱SÁNEĆ Territory, July 2022

I helped to tie up their boats when they arrived. There were two, each carrying six people. The first one out to stand on the dock, about my height, a little broader, held out his hand. "I'm Ron Peters," he said.

I took his hand and replied, "Harold Johnson. Welcome."

Turns out, Ron wasn't the organizer. He was just the first man out of the boat that afternoon. The organizer was Jim Toews, taller than Ron and me. He had a solid grip when he shook my hand—a man who did manual labour.

"Thanks for having us, Harold."

"No problem," I replied.

Ten more people climbed out of the aluminium boats, shed their life jackets, and came up the dock to stand in our front yard. I had never met any of them before. The Saskatchewan ecumenical society had emailed me to make the arrangements, and all I knew from the initial introductory message was that the society was made up of people from many faiths, including Christians, Buddhists, Muslims, Judaists, and members of First Nations. I was intrigued. Maybe there was a chance for humanity.

It was Cathy Wiens who had sent the original message. She said they were interested in meeting me because some of the people in the group had heard me speak. Others had seen videos circulating on YouTube. In *Firewater: How Alcohol is Killing My People (and Yours)* I had begun a discussion of the power of story. They were intrigued. They wanted to know more.

And now here they were, standing around in my front yard.

"Welcome, welcome." I waved them over to where I had started a fire and put out a few chairs.

"Thank you for coming. There are more of you than I expected. No matter, we can find a few more chairs.

"I want to thank you for coming. What a beautiful evening to sit around a fire and talk about stories. I'm especially happy to see that there are both Indigenous and non-Indigenous people here because what I have to say about stories is for everyone.

"Come on, everyone. Come and sit down. We have a long evening ahead of us."

They came. They brought out a few more chairs from the shed. Soon everyone was sitting in a circle around the fire I had started when I first heard the boats approaching.

This is what I told them.

THE POWER OF STORY

It has become common in situations like this to give what people are calling a land acknowledgement. Well, I want to do something like that as well. But I am not going to simply acknowledge the people who originally occupied this land, my ancestors the Nehithaw and our cousins the Metis. Instead, I want to acknowledge the actual land we are sitting on. All these trees, and that water over there, and this grass, and all the animals, and the birds, and everything else, and the spirits of this place, are all part of a shared story that we—Indigenous and non-Indigenous people alike— are included in. The land—us—the water—the sky— we're all part of one big, beautiful story.

This land we are on is where my grandfather settled after being evicted from the territory that became Prince Albert National Park. My mother was only twelve years old when the RCMP went there and told all the Indians they had to leave.

When they lived here, from about 1928 to about 1956, my grandfather's garden covered this entire area where we are sitting. About seventy years ago, he moved from here to be closer to town so the kids didn't have to walk or paddle so far to go to the school.

Joan and I came here about twenty years ago. It was all overgrown. We cleared the land and built our cabin and have been here ever since. It's a good place. To me it feels like home. That dock where you tied up your boats marks the beginning of the Montreal River. Everything south of the dock is Montreal Lake, everything north is river. It flows to La Ronge, about a three-day paddle from here.

A few hundred metres south is where the adhesion to Treaty Six was signed in 1889. But Indigenous people have been using this land for a lot longer than that. This was a well-known place to people who paddled the lake and river. It's the perfect stopping point.

We've had a couple of extreme water levels here in the last few years. Each time the lake floods, it erodes the bank a little more. After the first flood, I was walking the beach and found what looked to me to be flakes left by someone working stone. The next flood, I found a complete arrowhead. Most interestingly, I found a piece of chert, used commonly in stone tool making. The closest place to find chert is in Montana.

In my mind, Indigenous people have been stopping here for ten thousand years or more. So imagine that: where you are sitting, thousands of years ago someone sat in the same spot and flaked stone to make hunting arrows.

I want to thank Rosella for introducing me. You've followed protocol. You asked to come here. You gave me a gift. That's a really nice blanket. Thank you. I think it's going to come in handy before long, once the sun goes down and it starts to cool off.

But now I'd like to introduce myself, and introduce the idea of lifestory.

I was raised here. This used to be a community of trappers and fishers. Growing up, I heard all the stories of trapping and fishing and believed I could become a trapper and fisher.

My father died when I was eight years old, and my mother, with six children to look after, took over trapping and fishing. When I was about thirteen, I was walking the trapline with her. It was a beautiful March day. We were walking on a frozen river. The sun was toward the southwest—so about two or three in the afternoon. The wind was warm and from that same southwest direction. The sky was clear with a few wispy clouds. I remember everything about those minutes, including the crunch of my mother's moccasins on the snow. It had melted and frozen and melted and frozen and sounded different. She stopped walking and said:

"Nikosis, you have to learn this. You have to learn how to trap, you have to learn how to fish, you have to learn how to make your living off the land in case anything ever happens to that other world."

I knew what she meant. I had heard her stories about the Great Depression.

The conversation lasted less than a minute, but for some reason it stuck. From then on, I made sure I could survive in both worlds. I'm not the best woodsman out here. There are people with greater skills than mine. But I can survive, and that has made all the difference.

When I was mining, I could tell a foreman to piss off. He could fire me. It didn't matter, because I knew I could survive. As I was telling my wife, Joan, that knowledge was what gave me the confidence to do all the things I have done, including going to Harvard. I remember the first thing I packed in my car before heading to Cambridge, Massachusetts, was my camping gear and my tent. Having them took away the anxiety of going somewhere I had never been before.

Those few words my mother spoke to me on the trapline when I was a teenage boy are a story that has shaped my life. Even now, all these years later, I still have matches or a lighter in my pocket, I have a Leatherman with a knife on my belt—just in case. They are my security blanket. I feel safe when I carry them.

When I was about seventeen, a man from my community came back from Cyprus and Egypt. He had been a peacekeeper and told me stories about being in the Canadian Armed Forces. Hearing those stories, I was able to imagine myself in the military. I joined the Canadian Navy as a marine engineer. In the military I learned all the songs and stories of Maritime Command. The story I told myself was, "I am a hard-working, hard-drinking sailor man."

My older brothers had been working as loggers and miners. When I got out of the navy and returned to Northern Saskatchewan, I heard their stories about mining and logging, and for the next several years I worked in camps across Northern and Western

Canada. Everything I owned fit in a packsack, and my home was a bunkhouse. I told myself, "I am a hard-working, hard-drinking, tough son-of-a-bitch logger, miner, sailor—don't fuck with me." I wasn't putting anyone on. That's who I believed I was.

I met a woman, got married, had children, and my story changed. I became the hard-working-provider-protector. If I had dropped the hard-ass part of my story, my marriage might have survived.

I didn't.

Nineteen ninety-one. I was working at the Key Lake uranium mine as a heavy-equipment operator. There was a story going around that said if you drove a dozer or a haul truck, you were stupid. To prove I wasn't stupid, I quit mining and went to university. I picked the hardest thing they had. I picked law. Not because I wanted to be a lawyer. I was there to prove a point. Harold Johnson isn't stupid.

When you are Aboriginal and get a degree in anything, there is a story that says, "You didn't earn that. They just gave it to you, because you are an Indian." To prove no one gave me anything, I went to Harvard and got a master's degree in law. Then for twenty years I was stuck being a lawyer.

Early on in my legal career, I was defence counsel. I told myself that I was protecting Aboriginal people in the justice system. Then I became a Crown prosecutor and told myself that because all the victims of crime in this territory were Aboriginal, I was protecting the victims. I told myself that story until it didn't make sense anymore. I quit being a lawyer, resigned from prosecutions, and withdrew from the law society.

The point of all of this, other than to introduce myself, is to show the power of story. Every time I changed the story I was telling myself, my life changed, sometimes in a fundamental way. What I just told you is what I call my lifestory. I am the author of it, and the editor.

You came here to sit around this fire and talk about story. Maybe you thought I was going to tell stories, maybe you thought I was going to teach you how to write stories. I'm not sure what you thought you were going to get. But this is what I want to talk about. This is what I think is important about stories. We become the stories we are told and the stories we tell ourselves. The important story is our own lifestory. That story isn't independent from the stories dominant society tells us. There is an intermingling of my lifestory and the stories available to me, and the shared stories that structure our society put real limits on the stories I am able to tell myself.

But it is through my lifestory that I am able to experience the tremendous power of story. This is where I can make change, and that change can influence the larger stories. Right now we are in transition between the industrial era and the technological era. The dominant story is changing, and this is when we can make a difference. We can impact the stories we share, but only if each of us first has control over our own lifestory.

We are all story. We are the stories we are told and we are the stories we tell ourselves. To change our circumstances, we need to change our story: edit it, modify it, or completely rewrite it. You have your lifestory. It's the story you tell yourself about yourself. It's as true as any other. If you tell yourself a story over and over again, no matter how improbable it may sound when you begin, in time the story will manifest itself.

Stories are not *part* of your culture. Your culture is story. It is entirely story. Everyone's is. We are all the stories we are told. Our being is story. Our essence is story. Our vision is shaped by story; our hearing, our morals and ethics are all story. The wiring in our brains is shaped by story. Every thought you think is framed by story.

I am story.

You are story.

The universe is story, and it all comes from the Trickster.

None of the stories we tell ourselves are true. We've made them up. It wasn't intentional. We simply inferred meaning into the experiences we encountered. Shortly after my birth, someone put a nipple in my mouth and squirted warm milk. At the same time, I heard sound. My brain connected the sound I was hearing with the taste of warm milk in my mouth—a neural pathway was created, and I inferred meaning to my experience. I connected the taste of my mother's milk with the sound of her voice. My mother's voice was a story that meant I was cared for. As I grew, I continued to infer meaning into my experiences. Each new experience built upon previous experiences. I interpreted them, I inferred meaning into them, based upon what was already in my body of understanding. That is to say, upon previous inferences.

A child learns an amazing amount in its first years. I learned a language. I learned the rules of socialization. I learned mobility and balance. I learned to walk and talk and think. I learned things adults struggle with. I learned how to imagine, how to play, how to pretend. Each bit of learning, as I developed my understanding of who I was, where I was, and who I was related to, built upon previous understandings. I interpreted new experiences based upon what was already in my brain, and I continued to add to that body of understanding throughout my life, through grade school, then high school, into the world of work, through marriage and parenthood, into university, and throughout my career as a lawyer and writer, and now as an Elder.

Each time I came upon new information, I inferred meaning into it based upon what I had already learned. I interpreted the world around me based upon a core body of understanding that I continuously grew.

This is different from assuming meaning. Assumptions are conclusions based upon belief. Most racist ideas are assumptions. Inferences, on the other hand, are conclusions based upon an interpretation of the evidence available—not based purely on belief.

I hope I relied, and still rely, more upon inference than I did upon assumption, but I am human and humans err. Some of what I think I know is merely assumed, based in belief, and might be wrong. But even if I didn't make any assumptions—if my interpretation of the world around me was pure inference—it still is likely wrong. This is because the act of inferring, of interpreting experience and evidence, relies upon knowledge that is already in my mind. Everything in my mind is a chain of inferences going all the way back to the taste of warm milk in my mouth and my mother's voice. If anywhere along that chain, I inferred wrongly—if I interpreted an experience or evidence poorly—then everything that follows is informed by an idea that isn't true.

Here's an example. Early on in life I came to the conclusion that hard work was essential to my purpose. I allowed it to define who I was. Being a hard worker won me respect and accolades, which in turn reinforced my belief in the importance of hard work.

I should have figured it out while I was in the midst of it. For a time I worked one week in a remote mine camp, followed by one week at home. Except I didn't spend the week at home. Instead, I ran a small forestry operation. I worked extremely hard. Harder than anyone I knew, and yet I lived not very far above the poverty line. Hard work on its own does not ensure success. I lost my forestry operation when Canada Revenue came after me for back taxes.

It's only now, as an Elder looking back, I can see how that faulty inference diminished my life. I spent too much time working and not enough time with my family. In real terms I would have been much richer if I had not pursued economic wealth over mental, emotional, and spiritual wealth.

The story I have been building throughout my life is probably a fiction in more ways than one. Knowing that I inferred wrongly at times as I built the chain of inferences that make up my understanding leads me to conclude that I cannot say with any certainty that anything is true.

And neither can you.

This conclusion is liberating. If we cannot with certainty say that anything is absolutely true, then we are not bound to any single version of the story we inhabit. We are free to change our story, modify it, amend it, or completely rewrite it. We are free to adopt any story we chose.

That means there is no such thing as non-fiction. Multiple stories can be told about any event. We choose which one to tell. For example: I told you that I went to Harvard because I wanted to prove that nobody gave me anything. That's true. But I also went to Harvard because Harvard is a prestigious place and I wanted some of that prestige. Another reason I went to Harvard was to study. I wanted to know more.

Without all of the details, and as you've seen with my Harvard story, when elements are missing, you only get one version of the story. When new information is added, the meaning of the story is changed.

Try to tell a completely true story of our gathering this evening. You would have to tell the thoughts of each person here. You would have to tell how they came to be here, and to tell each person's story accurately, you would have to tell the story of each of their family members. You would have to include the fire we are sitting around, how it was started, which wood was chosen, and the story of the tree the wood came from. For the story to be complete you would have to tell the history of this place going back 4.543 billion years and the story of everything that has ever happened here.

I know that's a bit extreme. I know what I am saying is impossible in practice. We try to tell whole stories by telling only the pertinent parts, and, out of necessity, we omit that which we consider irrelevant. But that's the point. We choose what we leave out. Like a carver, we shave off bits and pieces until we have the image we are looking for. While the image might be the best that we can create, it is still something that we created, and a created story is the very definition of fiction.

So nothing is true.

That's okay.

We're all living in fictions.

But fictions are pretty fantastic things.

When I was young my mother told us Wisahkicahk stories, how he re-created the world after the flood with a little bit of dirt brought up from the depths by Muskrat; how he tricked the ducks and geese into dancing with their eyes closed; and how in yet another story he ended up with a burned ass. What I loved about our Trickster was not only that there were many traditional stories about him, but that we could make up our own. It seems Wisahkicahk encouraged us to do so. He liked being famous.

So now I want to tell you the story I made up about Wisahkicahk.

Kayas, one day Wisahkicahk was watching television, and he saw an Indian Story on there. But the story didn't seem right. It was all mixed up.

He went to check on the original.

He had it somewhere.

The Creator gave Wisahkicahk a whole bag of stories back at the beginning of time and had told Wisahkicahk, "Here, look after these, the people are going to need them to know how to live a good life, and they are going to need them when times become difficult."

But Wisahkicahk couldn't find them.

Man, he was in trouble now.

He'd lost the stories the Creator had given him.

So he went looking for them, and he saw Buffalo, way off in the distance, just one by himself. Wisahkicahk walked over to him and said, "Hey, Paskwamostos, my brother. Have you seen that bag of stories the Creator gave me? I think I lost them."

Buffalo shook his big shaggy head. He said, "Nooooooh, sorry, Wisahkicahk. I don't see much anymore. They keep me here in the park, and people come to look at me. I don't get around like I used to. Nooooooh, I didn't see where you left your stories."

"Oh, that's too bad," Wisahkicahk said, and went on looking for his stories.

He saw Wolf running away from him. Wisahkicahk shouted, "Hey, Mahikan! My brother, stop. Wait. Why are you running away?"

Wolf stopped and came back. "I try to stay away from people now. Every time I come close, they shoot at me or try to poison me. What can I do for you, Wisahkicahk?"

"I lost that bag of stories the Creator gave me. You didn't happen to see them, did you?"

"No, sorry, older brother," Wolf answered. "No, I'm sorry, I never saw your stories; like I said, I keep away from people now."

Wisahkicahk kept looking. Next, he saw Bear digging around in a garbage pit. He shouted down to him. "Hey, Maskwa, my brother. What are you doing down there?"

Bear answered, "This is where I eat now. There's no forest left, there are no berries."

"Oh well, I guess that's the way it is. You didn't by chance happen to see where I left that bag of stories the Creator gave me, now, did you? I seem to have misplaced them."

"No, sorry, Wisahkicahk. I never saw them. But maybe you never lost them. Maybe someone stole them, like they steal my claws and my gallbladder."

That made sense to Wisahkicahk. Of course, someone stole them. That must be what happened. That's how they ended up on that television.

He looked up, and there was Bald Eagle flying. He yelled up at her, "Hey Mikisiw, my sister."

She circled around and around and slowly came down. When she landed in a tree just above Wisahkicahk, he said, "Sister, you can see far. You can see the future, and you can see the past. Did you see who stole that bag of stories the Creator gave me back at the beginning of time?"

"Yes, I did, Wisahkicahk," she answered. "While you were watching television in the twentieth century, Fox stole your stories."

"Ohhhhh yeah, that makes sense."

So, Wisahkicahk went looking for Fox, and he found him, and Fox had that bag of stories. He was dragging it around. Wisahkicahk knew he could never catch Fox. Fox was too fast, he could turn too quickly, and if Wisahkicahk chased him, maybe the stories would get hurt.

So, he followed him, and he found one of the stories. It had fallen out of the bag. Fox had dragged those stories around for so long that he had worn a hole in the bag.

Wisahkicahk picked up that story. It was almost dead. Its fur was all matted and dirty, and it was barely breathing. It just lay there in Wisahkicahk's hands with its eyes closed. It was the dream catcher story.

Wisahkicahk gently brushed the dirt off it. Then he blew on it. Blew a little bit of life into it.

Slowly that story began to revive.

Wisahkicahk blew on it some more. Every time he blew on it, the dream catcher story became a little bit stronger.

Finally, that little story opened its eyes. It wasn't completely recovered yet. But Wisahkicahk had a plan.

He used that story to make a whole bunch of dream catchers. They weren't very good because the story was so weak—but they were good enough. He sold them, and he sold his buckskin jacket that he didn't wear anymore, and he sold his moccasins, and he used that money to buy the biggest big screen TV he could find.

Then he took that big screen TV into the forest, and he plugged it into a currant bush.

And then he hid and waited.

Sure enough.

Along came Fox.

Curious Fox. He stopped to watch that big TV, and when he was completely hypnotized by it . . . Wisahkicahk stole back that bag of stories so that the people would again know how to live a good life.

The reason our stories have humour is because people put shields up in front of themselves. When we make them laugh, their shields come down, and we can slip in the message of the story. That's also why we sit in a circle. If we sit across from each other, the shields we hold in front of ourselves get in the way. The best way to communicate with someone is to sit side by side—that way our shields don't block our communication. When we are in a circle like this, we are all sitting beside each other. We are all equal.

We are all facing a warm fire, we're comfortable, we're relaxed. Check out this light. Just look around and take it in. I love the light this time of day. It's so soft compared to the harshness of midday.

How did we get here?

Yeah, I know, you came by boat this afternoon.

I'm talking about how *we* got to this place in history. What thread did we follow?

We collectively create stories, fictions, knowing they are fictions, knowing they represent only one version of reality, and we use these stories to create our social world. We just make shit up. In his wonderful first book *Sapiens: A Brief History of Humankind*, Yuval Noah Harari explains that we create fictions to facilitate society. After hundreds of thousands of years as hunter-gatherers, humans began to experiment with agriculture only about ten thousand years ago. We had previously governed our societies in groups of no more than a hundred or a hundred and fifty people, through familial relationships and what Harari calls gossip—I think this word means something different than the important information-sharing he's talking about. But agricultural societies were much larger and needed a bigger story to hold them together. So we invented religion.

Harari's argument accounts for the history of the last few thousand years, during which we see religion facilitate authority. God's word was not to be questioned. The interpreters of God's word assumed God's authority, and so society was governed by the priest class. Until only a couple of centuries ago, monarchs claimed to rule as direct descendants of Adam, the first man. They claimed that God's grant to Adam of dominion over the world was passed down to them through lineage. People had to believe the Genesis story in order to accept the monarch story. Each story was built upon previous stories.

We no longer accept that monarchs have God's permission to rule. That story changed. Prior to stumbling upon the Americas, European people lived in feudal systems that were rigidly hierarchical and highly authoritarian. The system wasn't questioned because no one imagined a different way of being. To those people, hierarchy and authority were natural, normal, and necessary. When they learned, through people like John Locke, that in the Americas, people lived without monarchs, without kings and princes and courts and judges and force, it blew their minds. They began to imagine for themselves a society without kings and princes.

It was a dangerous time. A world order was beginning to collapse. People started to imagine anarchy, that they could live without authority. Then authority was saved by Locke. He could see that the monarchy had to be abandoned, that the story supporting it had unwound. But his social order could be saved through a new story. In his *Two Treatises of Government*, which throughout his life he denied writing, only becoming known as its author after his death, Locke defends his social order by viciously attacking American Indigenous Peoples. *Two Treatises of Government* is one of the most racist things I have ever read. Yet despite its blatant racism and complete fabrications, that work became the heart of modern Western society. It forms the basis of the United States Constitution.

Thank you, young man for putting more wood on the fire. It really is starting to cool down, isn't it.

There is a story going around about how we got to be here, collectively, in this place in history. The story tells us Europeans came to Turtle Island and colonized the original inhabitants—that they destroyed our culture—eradicated our language—removed us from the land and dispossessed us of our relationship with the Creator. The colonization story informs most of what people have to say about Indigenous Peoples. It is our rallying cry. It is what we resist.

Let me tell you a variation of the colonization story, with some different details included.

The reason Christopher Columbus went looking for India was because he wanted a new trade route to perfume and spices. The trade route in existence from China and India to the Europe of his time traversed the Middle East. This was a few hundred years after the Crusades, and the Europeans had made a lot of enemies there—enemies that taxed the caravans and drove up the prices.

Europe really isn't a continent. It is not separate from Asia. The division was created by Genghis Khan. Europe is the portion of the larger continent that Khan did not want. There was nothing there. All the wealth was in India and China.

What we now refer to as Europe had no advanced technology, no medicine, no science, and no art. It had been devastated by the bubonic plague and its population was poor and dirty.

Even wealthy Europeans who could afford meat did not have technology to preserve it. That's why they wanted spices. If you have to eat old meat, spices make it palatable.

European custom at the time did not include bathing. They had two baths in their life—once when they were born and again when they died. When a population stinks, perfume becomes important. So, the main reason Europeans stumbled upon the Americas in search of perfume and spice is because they stank and their food was rotten and tasted bad.

I see a few people squirming. It's not comfortable to hear negative stories about your history. We know how you feel. Negative stories about Indigenous people have been told to us for a long time, about how we were backward and childish and worshipped trees and rocks and needed Europeans to save us. The history that you are familiar with is one that has been sanitized for your benefit. It's your background story. It's told that way to make you feel good about yourself. What I am about to tell you is going to challenge that version. It's okay, you can hear it. You don't have to feel bad. It's just a story.

European societal structures were rigidly hierarchical. They had a lord in a castle at the apex and serfs at the bottom. Land was held in tenure. If you farmed this plot of land, it was because your father had farmed it, and his father had farmed it before him. They hadn't imagined ownership yet. That was to come. Everyone in that social structure had a place. You were born into your place and remained there throughout your life. The lowest people in the feudal system were lordless men. These were outlaws hiding in the forest, or merchants who walked between villages with packsacks filled with pots and pans.

When Columbus stumbled upon the Americas, he found food and medicines. Think about that picture of the first Thanksgiving. We are shown black-hatted Pilgrims and a table stacked with food—corn, beans, squash, pumpkin, potatoes, carrots, turnips, tomatoes, and turkey. All that food was American food, including the turkey. None of it was known in Europe, where wheat, oats, and barley were primarily grown. In the Thanksgiving picture, the Pilgrims share their bountiful harvest with the original inhabitants. The story it tried to tell is a perversion. It was the Aboriginal Peoples who shared their food with the Pilgrims to keep them from starving. The Pilgrims had come to the Americas because they did not have a place in Europe. They were outcasts who needed our help.

The very act of thanksgiving was a theft of Aboriginal culture. The Lakota wopila is a thanksgiving in which a person has a ceremony, then sponsors a feast and a giveaway. By being generous and giving gifts, the person expresses their thanks to the Creator. The Potlatches celebrated on the West Coast is another form of thanksgiving that involved feasting and gift-giving. The Lakota wopila tradition, which I follow, can occur at any time of the year. Whenever I feel like giving thanks, I can sponsor a feast and a giveaway. To agricultural societies, like our relatives in the east, the Iroquois, and others, thanksgiving ceremonies reasonably occur in the autumn after a harvest. That major holiday in the Americas now celebrated by nearly everyone, not just farmers, is an idea borrowed from Aboriginal Peoples.

When this new healthy food that we shared with the Pilgrims was taken back to Europe, it helped to cause an increase in population. Remember their numbers had been severely reduced by the Black Death. New medicines from the Americas alleviated illness and pain. Europe began to grow and prosper.

Wealth from the Americas was transferred back to Europe on ships loaded with gold. Now keep in mind who had come to the Americas. Those tied to their castles couldn't leave, and those tied by tenure to the land couldn't leave. That left the outlaws, the outcasts, and the merchants. When this newly wealthy class returned to Europe, they had more money than the monarchs. The kings and princes and lords had been involved in continuous wars with each other for centuries, and now their treasuries were empty.

So, some of the lowest class of people became the richest, and the feudal system was turned upside down. This new wealthy class didn't own any land in Europe. Nobody did, because land was not owned. It was held in tenure. But when you have money, you can change the rules. Private ownership allowed the new rich to purchase land. They didn't buy it from the tenured tenants. They bought it from the lords, who were broke and needed money to refill their depleted treasuries. It didn't take much. They just changed the story about tenure and property. The philosophers and political thinkers of the time, Thomas Hobbes and John Locke and James Harrington, helped the process along by making up theories of private property.

The lords kicked the tenants out and sold the land because, in the new property story, the lords owned the land. The tenants didn't have anywhere to go, so they immigrated to the Americas.

Five hundred years after Columbus, his Europe and the feudal system he came from has been obliterated. It has completely collapsed. Nothing of it remains.

So now we have powerful stories about private property, and we forget that these are recent stories, newly created, that we just made them up. These stories about private property are so powerful that a farmer in Saskatchewan was able to get away with killing a young Indigenous man because the jury at his trial believed the defence-of-private-property story.

Can someone get me a cup of that tea, please.

My throat's getting a little dry.

Thank you.

I live on the land here. That cabin behind us, I and my wife built it by ourselves. I fish and trap and gather from the forest. I know my relationship with the Earth. I participate in ceremonies that celebrate and communicate with the Creator. Aboriginal languages are still spoken here and are recovering. We've been through some rough times, but we know who we are, where we came from, and our place and purpose on this planet.

So, who colonized whom? It seems to me that we did more to change the European than the European did to change us.

What I have just told you is just another version of the colonization story. Which do you prefer: the one where Aboriginal people are victims, where we were unfairly made to change and adapt to the standards of the invader, or the version that says we made them who they are?

Neither version is absolutely true. No story can be. You get to choose which one you will adopt, which version will you tell yourself, tell your children, and tell your grandchildren.

We've struggled with the dominant story the colonizer has been telling us about our place here. In that story Canada is a sovereign nation and our people are not. We call ourselves First Nations Peoples, but at law, both domestic and international, we lack the capacity of sovereignty.

Sovereignty is just a story. A man named Francisco de Vitoria made it up around 1532.

Forty years after Columbus landed, the Spanish bragged that they had already killed over 12 million Aboriginal people. The rest of Europe was disgusted with them. There was a debate going on as to whether or not we were humans. It was a serious question with serious consequences. If we were in fact human, then their law precluded them from taking our stuff. If we were not human, they were free to discover and keep all our lands and belongings. Pope Paul III settled the matter in 1537 with a papal bull that declared we were humans and we had a right to keep our stuff.

In 1532, when Vitoria gave his speeches on making war on the Indians, the question of our humanity was still open. He came up with the idea of sovereignty just in case we were humans after all. He defined sovereignty by looking at the European states in existence at the time. His definition of sovereignty is simply a description of the European nation state of his day. He said that if a state had a defined territory, exclusive occupation of that territory, and had a prince—then it was sovereign. If it didn't have those attributes—it wasn't. Of course, his definition excluded Aboriginal Peoples' relationship to the land, and we were therefore deemed not to be sovereign states. Since we were not sovereign, they could take our stuff, whether or not we were human.

Stories are powerful. Vitoria didn't even write this one down. We know about it because students in attendance at his lectures took notes. The story had tremendous power because it defined something that hadn't been defined before. Never mind that it was completely made up—that it was pure fiction—it caught on.

In 1580 the king of Sweden realized that he claimed all of Sweden but did not occupy the northern portion. Occupation was suddenly important. It was an element of this new thing called sovereignty. So, he asked people from Finland to come to northern Sweden and occupy it on his behalf. He promised them free land and no taxes for six years.

The newcomers practiced swidden agriculture. They chopped down the forest and burned the trees, thereby putting nutrients into the soil. They did not have enough rye—the only seed they brought with them—the first year and had to wait until the second year before they could eat their crop. They relied upon hunting, fishing, trapping, and gathering to survive and became known as the Forest Finns. They lived communally, worked together, and helped each other. They made their living from the land through agriculture and keeping a few animals, sheep and cows, and continued to fish, trap, hunt, and gather from the surrounding forest. They made their money by making and selling guns. The soil there contains a lot of iron and grass brings up the iron, which is deposited on its stems and leaves. The Forest Finns gathered the grasses that grow in marshes. They burned the grass and smelted the iron.

I know about the Forest Finns because they are my father's ancestors. He was born in Sweden in 1898. The sovereignty story is part of his story.

My father's father, John Olaf Jonsson, was convinced to move to Canada because of that same sovereignty story. Canada claimed this land from coast to coast but did not sufficiently occupy the prairies. Without occupation and clear sovereign title, there was a risk the Americans would move in and take it for themselves. So, Canada enticed Europeans to come and settle the prairies on its behalf with promises of almost-free-land and opportunities. My grandfather immigrated to southern Saskatchewan in 1907 and was granted a homestead on a half section of land.

The irony of this story is that I sometimes hear Aboriginal people adamantly argue that we are sovereign—that we are sovereign states—that we are nations. We cannot be sovereign. We can never be sovereign. Sovereignty means: except Aboriginal Peoples. The concept was created to exclude us.

Sovereignty might be a made-up story, but it is a powerful one. Not only is it responsible for mass migrations, it is responsible for horrendous acts of domination, of murder, rape, and pillaging, of dispossession and subjugation. Vitoria's little story has caused wars. It has become the basis of international law. The story he made up has led to the insane belief in nationalism. It is the story relied upon by our oppressors to validate their occupation of our territory. But despite its overwhelming acceptance by our oppressors and even by our own people, sovereignty is nothing but a made-up story. It's an example of how powerful stories are, a reminder that we must be careful of the stories that we tell. We don't know what impact they might have five hundred years in the future.

·

As an Indigenous person, I do not rely upon Vitoria's story to understand my place. I have my own understanding of my relationship here. My father was a Swede and my mother was Nehithaw. My Indigenous ancestors, the ones I identify with most strongly, lived upon this land. When they died their bodies were placed upon scaffolds, wrapped tightly in buffalo robes. The birds ate at them, the scaffolds rotted and fell down, the worms took pieces of my ancestors down into the earth. My ancestors' atoms are in the land. The plants reached down with their roots and took up those atoms and brought them back to the surface. Deer, rabbits, and moose ate those plants, and my ancestors' atoms are in those animals. My ancestors' atoms are in the berries and mushrooms and medicines I gather. When I eat those berries and the meat of the animals, my ancestors' atoms are in me. When I die, I will be buried, and I will go back to the earth, the worms will eat me and spread my atoms, and the cycle will repeat itself.

I do not say that we are sovereign. I do not say that the land belongs to us, because to do so would be to buy into the fiction of property. Instead, I say, I belong here. I belong to the land. I am the land. I am this place.

Those of you here this evening who are not Aboriginal are probably wondering about your relationship to the land. I have a story about that.

When treaties were negotiated with us, my great-grandfather James Ross was there. He told my mother and my mother told me what was said. We did not sell our land. We could not. We never saw ourselves as owners. What we did was share. We adopted the settlers as our relatives in an adoption ceremony. By being adopted, they obtained the right to be here.

Adoption is one of the seven ceremonies that are connected to the Sacred Pipe. I am going to tell you a very abbreviated version of the adoption ceremony story here. If you want the complete story you will have to go to someone who has it and go through the proper protocols to hear it. A Lakota man went on a vision quest and had a vision of corn. When he came back, he went looking for the thing he saw in his vision. He found it, and he brought it back to his people. The people who had grown the corn followed him. They said, "That's our corn." The man said, "It must be our corn, because I saw it in a vision." They could have gone to war, but instead they adopted each other. Now we adopt each other as brothers and sisters, and we can adopt parents and grandparents, but the first adoption ceremony in our culture was one Nation adopting another.

At the beginning of negotiations of the numbered treaties, the treaty commissioner Alexander Morris smoked the Sacred Pipe with us. He understood that he was entering into ceremony, though he might not have appreciated its power. More likely he was trying to be diplomatic. Merely going along, so as to be seen participating. He twisted things to his advantage. He used the words "as long as the sun shines, the rivers flow, and the grass grows." Which to my ancestors at the treaty negotiations meant that he was calling on those powerful spirits, the sun, the grass, and the rivers, to witness the ceremony. Morris frequently referred to "Our Mother the Queen" and "Brother to Brother relationship." We were confident that he understood the treaty was an adoption ceremony. Morris might not have understood it this way, but to my ancestors sitting and listening to him, it seemed as though he did. To us, the Nehithaw, we were adopting the Queen's children and agreeing to share this territory with them.

As our relatives, the settler people obtained the right to gather from the forest, the right to dig for minerals, the right to build their towns and villages, their cities and their roads. All the wealth that the settler people obtained from this land—the oil and gas, the uranium, the lumber, the gold and copper and nickel and iron—they got the right to use through their relationship with Indigenous Peoples. As our relatives they became equal with us. All the rights that Canadians enjoy, all the privileges they have living in one of the wealthiest countries in the world, are Treaty Rights. They got the right when they were adopted in the ceremony of treaty-making. They have those rights by virtue of being related to Indigenous Peoples. When we adopted them as our relatives, as our cousins, our ancestors became their ancestors.

When our new cousins' atoms are in the soil, when their grandchildren eat the plants and the animals and have their ancestors' atoms in them, then the settler will completely belong here. Maybe they will learn to love the land more than they love what they take from it.

I am told to call the settler people kiciwamanawak. It means "our cousins." It means all of us are cousins to all of them. As cousins, we should respect each other, help each other, live side by side—not interfere in each other's way of being.

All of us sitting around this fire this evening are family. We are related. None of us has a superior right to be here. We can make up stories about sovereignty, about the Crown's underlying title, about land ownership—but they are just stories. Only the worms know the truth, and they are waiting for us regardless of which story we choose to tell ourselves. Eventually we are all going to belong to this land.

Yeah, this is the time of evening when the mosqui-tos come out. If someone would throw a piece of green wood on the fire, the smoke will help keep them away.

No, thanks. I will use insect repellent if they get really bad. Until then, I just tolerate them. They're not too bad out here in the open by the lake. I assure you, if you walk back into the trees any distance, you will find many more. Or, I guess I should say, they will find you.

We are in a new age. Yeah, we are all sitting here around a fire and the sun is going down and the mosquitos are beginning to come out, and everyone has their cell phones shut off. I don't see anyone with their head down, looking into their hands, checking the latest status updates. But even though we have put them aside for the time we are here, we are undoubtedly fully in the age of the cell phone. If you look across the lake—there—up in the hills, that red light. That's a cellular tower. The bandwidth here is a little low, reception isn't great, but we are covered.

With the invention of the transistor in 1947, we left behind the industrial era and entered the information age. Developments in transistor technology allowed the computer to shrink so that now your cell phone has more computing power than the computer used by NASA to put the first men on the moon. Our lives have been fundamentally and forever changed, and the change has been rapid. Consider that the Wright brothers first flew in 1903, the transistor was invented in 1947, and we landed men on the moon in 1969—only sixty-six years after we first took to the skies.

We are in a new age, and we need a new story. We need a story that will tell us who we are at this time in history, that includes all the new things we have learned, that tries to be more complete and doesn't leave anybody out. The old stories from the last age can't tell us what we are supposed to be doing now, nor what our purpose is.

Remember that the religion story facilitated the agrarian revolution. The invention of the steam engine, coupled with the wealth pilfered from the Americas, brought about the Industrial Revolution, and a new story was required to facilitate this massive societal upheaval. We came up with two: capitalism and socialism. Despite their alleged contradiction, they are both industrial stories. Both encourage the land-based serf to leave the farm and move into the city to work in factories. Both promise to improve the life of the worker. Capitalism, in theory, allows him to work

his way up a proverbial ladder of success with a promise that with hard work and luck, he, too, can become a
tycoon. Socialism promised the serf freedom to work
in a factory, a decent salary, benefits, and a pension.
Both the capitalist and socialist stories depend upon
the exploitation of the Earth's resources. A capitalist will cut down the last tree if there is money to be
made. A socialist will cut down the last tree so long as
the worker doing the cutting belongs to a trade union.
They are just two of the many stories we are telling
ourselves now, stories from which we derive our con-
scious world, our understanding of ourselves, and our
understanding of our place here.

Some of our stories, like the story about rights,
are so powerful that some people are prepared to
kill other people to protect their interpretations of
them. Rights don't exist in nature. Rights are stories
we made up. I've heard some pretty bizarre claims of
right—the right to not wear a mask during a pandemic,
the right to say horrible things about people on social
media, the right to a gun. When asked where these
rights come from, we often hear they came from God.
They didn't. The best claim to a right is that it exists
in legislation.

The *Charter of Rights and Freedoms* is a beautiful
story. It should win the Governor General's Award
for fiction. It's okay. The *Charter*, despite its fictional

nature, is the best we can do right now. When we organize our society, we can use stories about rights. They help to balance things. They only become a problem when people begin to believe that these stories we call rights are somehow fundamental, that they exist separate from us, and that they need to be defended with violence.

Another story, told by fundamentalists, is the one about evil. It's just a story. We made it up. It exists nowhere other than in our minds. In our original Nehithaw way of understanding, everything was good and bad at the same time. We don't get the separate concept of evil unless we create a dichotomy—when we break what we see in nature into two and make them opposites. It doesn't do us any good to do that; it serves no useful purpose. The concept of separate good and evil drives division and conflict. It gives us something to fight against. We can name a thing or a people evil and go to war against them.

Evil does not exist in nature. Look around you. There is nothing you can point to and say, "That is evil." A bear takes a fish, an eagle scavenges roadkill—these are natural acts, neither good nor bad. In the modern world, it is hard to say what is good and what is evil. The Aswan Dam in Egypt helped farmers irrigate, but because it reduced the nutrients that flowed down the

Nile into the Mediterranean Sea, the sardine fishery fell from 18,000 tons in 1962 to 460 tons in 1968. The dam might have been good for the farmers, but it was an evil for the fishers. People come from all across Canada to work in the tar sands. To them, employment and high wages are a good thing. To Aboriginal people living downstream and subjected to higher rates of cancer as a result, the tar sands are a death sentence. You might think that after working in the criminal justice system for two decades that I would have encountered a few evil people. I assure you I have not. I met some people who were so unhealthy they were a danger to themselves and to others, but I never met anyone I would classify as evil.

Even things we believe are absolute fact are merely the best story we can tell about ourselves right now. Science not only has its basic tenets rooted in story, it is essentially a story-generating machine. The original Christian story placed man at the centre of the universe. Copernicus changed that story to one where the planet Earth orbits the sun. Newton retold the orbiting planets story to include gravity. Einstein modified the story about gravity with the story of relativity. Quantum physics retells the story in impermanence. The Higgs boson story gives solidity to the impermanence. Fifty years from now, the story will change yet again when new ideas replace existing ones. Fifty years after that, the story will change yet again when even newer ideas emerge. At any given time—past, present, or future—the best science can do is to give us the most compelling story available about ourselves, our planet, and our place in the universe. No matter how compelling the story, we should know that it is not the incontrovertible truth. At some point in the future, the story, the truth we rely upon today, is going to change. It will be replaced by a new story.

That the best science can do is provide a coherent story does not diminish the validity of science. That the story is inevitably going to change in the future doesn't change the fact that the story science provides today is the best possible story available. We can still rely upon the story science provides to make decisions while knowing the basis of our decision is only the best presently known.

Think about it this way. I like working on old vehicles and have kept a few antiques running. When these vehicles were built, they were the best available. Then it was quite common to pull the points out of a distributor and use a bit of sandpaper to clean them up. They were easy to work on and easy to replace because they were designed to burn out. Yeah, there was a condenser to reduce the rate of burning, but it didn't eliminate it, and eventually you had to replace the points. Now the best available, our current, modern vehicles don't have points. They have electronic ignition, but even that is on its way out as we move to electric vehicles and the best available is shown again to be just that: what we have right now.

Science textbooks are good collections of stories, and the subjects of scientific studies are likewise story. The universe itself is possibly made from story. We know that the foundational building blocks of all matter, even dark matter and antimatter, are made from quanta, discrete units of energy that we've named quarks. In their normal state, subatomic particles are in superposition until they are observed. They are in effect everywhere and nowhere at the same time. Upon observation the particle collapses to a single point. This is known as the observer effect.

If we apply the concept of the observer effect to everyday reality, then the universe exists because we are aware of it. Albert Einstein did not agree. He famously asked if that meant the moon was not there when he was not looking at it. Despite Einstein's doubts, the evidence keeps piling up that the universe exists because it is part of our story. It's possible that our combined consciousness generates the illusion of physical reality. The universe might exist because we have a story that says it does.

When I am talking about the universe, I'm not just talking about distant galaxies and ever-expanding space. Earth is part of the universe. I am part of the universe. The Earth's biota, every living thing, you, me, everything, potentially exists because of story. At least, that is what the science story seems to be telling us.

Science is a story, but so, too, is its supposed antithesis—God.

Remember what I said before: organized religion has been used to hold societies together for at least ten thousand years. The God of the Old Testament seems designed by agriculturalists to explain problems like drought and pestilence. The New Testament Christian theology seems to admit that God is a story. It starts out, "In the beginning was the Word, and the Word was with God, and the Word was God."

The admission that God is words and hence a story does not diminish the concept of God. Words are very powerful. Stories are very powerful. They generate the illusion we experience as reality. The realization that God is story enhances the concept of God because it takes God out of the realm of the physical, absolute world and places him in the infinite possibility only available in story. Compare two concepts: God is a rock. God is the story that made rocks possible. My understanding of this first verse of the Gospel of John—"In the beginning was the Word"—is that it puts spirit into the concept of God. It changes the story of the old man with a beard, sitting on a golden throne dropping manna with one hand and throwing lightning bolts with the other, into a story of infinite possibilities.

We've only relatively recently begun to understand physical reality. Science has only been around for about five hundred years. It has evolved nicely. But even with its exponential growth, it cannot be expected to understand a universe 13.772 billion years old. In an infinite universe, there will always be infinite unknowns. In this realm of infinite possibility exists God, the Great Spirit, the Creator, the Great Mystery—not only the unknown, but also the unknowable. We might pride ourselves in our intelligence, but compared to what is potentially understandable, we know only a minuscule amount. I am definitely not an atheist. I accept that there are powerful forces at play that are beyond human comprehension. But I am not bound by a narrow biblical conception of God, a single story about him.

I think I am going to stop for a moment and get a cup of tea.

Oh, you haven't tried it yet? It's very nice. Some wild mint from down by the shore, some Labrador tea from behind the cabin, and just a pinch of catnip from the garden. It's quite soothing. I need it to lubricate my throat after all the talking.

At this point, all I am doing is giving you a list of things that are story—things you might not think about as story—things you might have considered natural, normal, and necessary. If you can imagine God, science, and the universe as story without diminishing them, then we've laid the groundwork for other concepts.

I'm just going to rattle off a few more examples. Some of them might be convincing, maybe not. It's okay. I'm giving you a lot of stuff here. Take what you can use in a good way. If you can't use what I am saying in a good way, leave it here. It's up to you.

Now where was I?

Oh yeah, I was talking about God.

God is a dynamic story, and so are we.

DNA (deoxyribonucleic acid) is an alphabet to write life with. Francis Crick, James Watson, and Maurice Wilkins won the Nobel Prize in 1962 for their discovery of the double helix blueprint of living cells. DNA is a four-letter alphabet: A, T, G, and C. With those four letters, we can write the story of every living thing on the planet. When we understand DNA, when we understand its language, when we can read its story—we will understand life. We've already begun to rewrite the story of life using this four-letter alphabet in genetic modifications of plants and animals.

The story of life is ancient and complex. We've just started to read it, to understand its language. When we understand this story, we will understand each other, because embedded in the lifestory is the story about how we are all related. And not only are all humans related, we are related to all the other life forms we share this planet with. Almost 99 percent of human DNA is identical to chimpanzee DNA. We also share 80 percent of our DNA with dogs, 60 percent with bananas, 50 percent with cabbage, and 16 percent with lettuce. The DNA story explains how we are related to every other life form on this planet at a cellular level. It's an important story—one we should pay attention to.

As Aboriginal people we have understood this for a long time—not the double helix, but that we are related to everything around us. It's part of our spirituality. When I finish saying a prayer, I remember to say "kakithaw nawakomakanak," which means, "all my relations." I am remembering that I am related to the being I am praying to and that I am related to every-thing around me: the Standing Nations of trees, the Four-Legged Nations, the Flying Nations of birds, the Swimming Nations of fish, and the Crawling Nations of insects. I remember that I am not more important than any other life form in nature.

Mathematics is story. Numbers are not real. They are merely useful concepts that we use to describe rela-tionships. Equations are sentences. Imagine $1+1=2$—the numbers are nouns, and the plus and equals signs are verbs. Equations are stories written in numbers that describe processes. $E=MC^2$ is a mathematical sto-ry: energy equals mass times the speed of light times the speed of light. Einstein first told this story well over a hundred years ago, and despite all the advances in quantum and astral physics, that story about energy, mass, and light has remained undisputed. The $E=MC^2$ story has survived so long that now it has become a legend.

DNA and mathematics are languages to tell stories with, and so is music. Some people are gifted music communicators, able to discern and produce sounds that transmit concepts of beauty, pleasure or even rage. The alphabet of music—do—re—mi—fa—so—la—ti or A, B, C, D, E, F, and G—is all that is needed to tell sto-ries not otherwise tellable. Songs, even without lyrics, are stories. The music itself expresses ideas of beauty, sadness, joy, and grief. Skilled musical communicators tell wordless stories that transmit ideas and concepts that even unskilled listeners can comprehend.

Good visual art is about storytelling. *The Scream*, by the Norwegian painter Edvard Munch, tells a story that evokes strong emotion. The story that infuses Mona Lisa's smile in Leonardo da Vinci's masterpiece is what makes this painting famous. Yes, his technical ability makes it possible to tell the story. But it's the story that then speaks to us. It's the story that we are left with.

Photography is the art of capturing story. A good photograph tells us something as much as it shows it. Yes, framing and light are important, but they are only important insofar as they capture and illuminate the story. If you are viewing good art, whether paint or photos, abstract or landscape, if it compels you to stop and ask yourself, "what's going on here?" then the artist has done a good job of capturing story.

Of course, movies and television are all about storytelling. But not just the dramas. Documentaries and news are also a form of storytelling. People who produce these shows know that the best way to get their message across is to encase it in story. Gifted documentary makers are also gifted storytellers.

Think about your education. Which teachers best imparted information to you? I'm sure if you think about it, you will conclude it was the best storytellers. The reason we learn so efficiently from storytelling is because we have been taught this way ever since our earliest ancestors sat around a fire in front of a cave and told stories about sabre-toothed tigers and ate mastodon. We've evolved this way over hundreds of thousands of years. Our brains are accustomed to organizing information into stories to make sense out of it. We can't do it any other way.

To think rationally is to follow a prescribed story outline. We take a new experience, new information, organize it into story, and if all the pieces fit, we conclude that the story is meaningful. It's just how our brains work. We do it automatically. Irrational thinking requires an editor to sort out the mess, to organize the words into sentences, and the sentences into a coherent structure.

When we go to sleep and go to the dream world, our brains take all the information we acquired during our waking period and organize it in story form. That is what a dream is—it's the story your brain made up using the information it gathered. The information is not just the stuff you saw and heard, it's also your thoughts and emotions—what you think and feel about everything you saw and heard. Your brain takes all of this and makes sense out it by fitting it into a story.

We live in Canada.

Except this country does not exist. Canada is an idea, a story that we tell ourselves. We have a constitution. It's in writing. We wrote it. We could have written anything we wanted. It's okay. It works. We use the story of the nation-state to organize ourselves. The story of the nation of Canada, like its predecessor, the feudal system story, provides a structure in which people find their place. The story speaks of defence, of economy, and of trade.

We tell ourselves a story about what it means to be Canadian. We create identities for ourselves. We tell ourselves, and the world, that we are kinder, gentler, more polite Americans. It's a good enough story. It includes hockey and maple syrup.

We have all been told the economy story repeatedly. We know that the money in our wallets is just pieces of paper. But the story about money is so powerful that people kill each other over those pieces of paper. The economy is a weave of stories. We once believed in dragons and unicorns. Now we believe in market forces.

The economy is supposedly premised upon supply and demand. Yet here in North America, a third of the food we grow is wasted—if it's not eaten, it's thrown away. At the same time, around the world, a child dies of malnutrition every three seconds. You'd think that people starving would create a demand that the supply would flow toward. It doesn't. You can demand all you want. If you don't have the money to pay for food, you die. The reason we don't send our excess food to the people who are starving is because it would impact the economy. The market would suffer. This story is so powerful that it demands human sacrifice. Some people on the planet must die to keep the market strong. Not all the dead are in some far-off country suffering from drought or war. We have undernourished children right here, living amongst us. We ignore them because we are caught up in the drama of the story we are telling ourselves about ourselves. Their deaths simply do not register.

Money is such a fiction that it transcends reality. Humans started out using seashells or sheep as currency, then adopted gold, silver, copper, or iron coins. The Chinese were the first to use paper money, essentially an IOU backed by the government. Eventually paper money became bank drafts and stocks and bonds. Now it's gone digital, and people have wallets on their mobile devices.

The amounts are massive: three trillion dollars move through the internet every day. That's not counting the billions hidden in crypto currencies. Now the newest economic story, the derivative, that ephemeral value obtained from the division of abstract capital, is in the marketplace. A quadrillion dollars' worth of derivatives trade every year in the stock market. That's a one with fifteen zeros behind it. It's a thousand trillion—a million billion—a billion million. That's ten times the value of every product manufactured worldwide during the last hundred years. Money isn't connected to the reality most of us experience anymore: buying groceries, buying a car, transactions in which one dollar is equal to something tangible. It's beyond imagination. It is pure speculative fiction.

Religion, science, nation, economy, currency: these are just starting points for a whole series of stories we tell ourselves.

Corporations are stories created by legislation that rely upon the Corporations Act for their very existence. But even though they are just stories, concepts we created, fictions given agency in the real world, corporations are believed by many to be natural, normal, and necessary. These fictions, these artificial entities, have been imbued with incredible wealth and power often greater than that of entire countries. Walmart is the tenth largest economy in the world, with revenues of $480 billion and over two million employees.

Walmart's economy is larger than that of Sweden or Norway or Russia.

Justice is a fiction. We created it. It's not something tangible. You can't touch it. You can't taste it. It's an idea. It's a story people made up. Justice doesn't exist in nature. A wolf kills an elk. An elephant knocks over a tree. A virus wipes out a population. None of the plants or animals or viruses invoke the principle of justice and demand redress.

The justice story we tell ourselves is based on punishment. Law enforcement attempts to correct wrongs and breaches of the law with punishment because the underlying story, the one told since the agricultural revolution, is based upon religion. The major religions of the world maintained order by threatening the populace with punishment by God. The story wasn't questioned, and it moved into the legal realm. The justice story is a retelling of the story about there being a judgement day.

The Supreme Court of Canada said that retribution was a hallowed principle of criminal justice. They pretty much said that vengeance was sacred and that God mandates the punishments the courts mete out. But punishment doesn't work. It's only used because people believe in it. The evidence shows that incarceration, the most common form of criminal punishment, does not deter criminality. Incarceration increases the likelihood that an offender will reoffend, it doesn't decrease it. Jails don't fix criminals. Jails make criminals. And so the justice system is self-perpetuating. It is in the business of creating criminals. That's the evidence. The persistent story, however, is that the justice system protects people from criminals.

Not only is justice something we made up, but so is the idea that there is such a thing as a justice system. After studying law for four years at law schools and more than twenty years practising it as a lawyer, I assure you there is no system. A system requires all the parts to communicate with each other and work together. The parts of the justice system don't. Judges don't talk to prison guards. Prosecutors don't talk to politicians. Law school professors tend to only talk to each other. There is no communication between the pieces. The story that there is such a thing as a justice system is a fiction. But the story serves a purpose. It allows people to think there is a coherent, consistent entity that can be blamed for society's failures or can hold society together. It helps them determine their place, and other peoples' places as well.

If we are paying attention, we know the justice system story is broken, that it does not work. Criminal law creates the criminal, and civil law is so time-consuming and expensive very few people can afford to use it. And those who can afford to use it don't. It takes far too long to bring an action through the courts. It can take decades to bring a lawsuit to conclusion. Businesses have adopted other means of settling disputes between themselves—faster, more efficient means.

So the courts are places where polluters and other wealthy culprits can hide from retribution. There are so many delays built into civil court procedures that big pharma, big oil, big tobacco, and alcohol corporations can tactically avoid judgement seemingly forever. And that's only when an action is commenced against them. They know that most of the people they hurt cannot afford to go to court against them, and so the justice system story does not deter them from hurting people to make a profit.

This isn't a modern failure. The common law has been around for a long, long time. The first criminal code was written by King Aethelberht in about 600 CE. So we've had this system of punishment for at least fourteen centuries, and never in that long history has it been shown to reduce crime.

People make up stories about how things work, then make up more stories that match up and fit together until there is a web of interwoven stories so complex they become the reality that constitutes society. Society is real. It has power over the people. It has norms and rules. It determines who lives and who dies, who is free and who is incarcerated. But this reality, this powerful control is made up of a series of fictional stories. They are entirely made up, one story modifying the last modifying the last, sometimes consciously and with intention and sometimes not. And because the stories are fictions, stuff we made up, the best version we had at the time, the stories can be changed.

No—no, thanks. I've had enough tea for now. I'm just going to wrap this nice blanket around my legs though. It really is getting cooler, isn't it?

Stories can heal and stories can kill.

Placebo: if a person is given a sugar pill and told the pill contains medicine, and if the person takes the pill and believes the medicine story, thirty to fifty percent experience a reduction in their symptoms. There was a young boy with leukemia who told himself a story about the Lone Ranger riding through his veins, shooting the cancer cells with silver bullets. He cured himself of leukemia.

There was a woman who was diagnosed with cancer. She didn't want to have cancer, didn't want to think about it. She went home and watched happy movies. One after the other, any movie, as long as it had a happy ending. Three months later she went back to the doctor, and her cancer was gone.

I've known these stories for a long time. I'm not sure where I first heard them. But anyone who looks for placebo stories will find many similar ones.

Stories can heal you.

Stories can kill you.

Nocebo: the opposite. Now the person is given the same sugar pill, but the story is that the pill contains poison. If the person takes the pill and believes the story, they will get sick and might even die. There was a young man, twenty-six years old, who took twenty-nine pills he believed were antidepressants. His heart rate slowed. His blood pressure dropped. He required medical intervention to stay alive, and he did not recover until he was told the pills he had taken were sugar pills.

There was another man with a very fast-acting cancer. He heard about a new wonder treatment and convinced his doctor to put him on it. Within a couple of weeks his tumour had shrunk. The wonder treatment worked. But then the man read a report that the treatment had been proven to be a fraud. His tumour began to grow again. The report was a nocebo. His doctor intervened and told the man that the report was inaccurate and the treatment actually did work, and gave him an injection and told him it was the treatment. It wasn't. It was a placebo—another story. The man believed the story and again the tumour quickly shrank. But the man eventually died. They could not maintain the story.

Stories can heal or kill. It's not just the pill. It's the story that accompanies its taking. Placebo and nocebo effects are not restricted to medicine and sugar pills. That might be where we are most familiar with them, but placebo and nocebo effects accompany every story. Every story we tell can heal or kill. You have to be very careful of the stories that you tell.

Augusto Monterroso is credited with writing one of the shortest stories. "El Dinosaurio (The Dinosaur)" is only eight words when translated into English. "Cuando despertó, el dinosaurio todavía estaba allí." ("When he awoke, the dinosaur was still there.") Despite its brevity, the story is complete. It lays out the barest of essentials—character, action, conflict—and the reader infers the rest. We infer that the *he* is a man. He might not be. He might be another dinosaur. We infer that the dinosaur was there before he went to sleep. It might not have been. It might have been in his dream. We find meaning in Monterroso's "Dinosaur" because we put meaning into it through our own inferences. We infer based upon the body of information we have stored in our minds. We interpret the story to make it consistent with what we already accept.

We make the story real, and that's where the power lies. Those eight words by themselves do not have all the meaning we put into them, all the power we give them. If the power of story was in the number of words, Monterroso's "Dinosaur" should have very little meaning.

Now think about this for a moment.

If eight words can possess all the power of a story, how short can a story possibly be?

How about two words—*racial trauma*.

Think about the lived experience of Indigenous people and other marginalized racial groups. Imagine having your skin abraded by the stares, by being followed in stores, by the silence when you enter a room, by the snide remarks, the constant interaction with people who treat you like you are something less while you know you have to work twice as hard as people in the dominant culture to achieve the same success, until your skin is so thin that everything hurts. Either that or your skin is so scarred, so calloused, that you don't feel anything at all anymore.

We can infer a lot of meaning into those two words. They encapsulate five hundred years of colonization.

I think one word can be a story.

Hope. What a desperate word.

Some of you here, when you were little girls and you sat on the lap of your kokum, your grandmother, she called you iskwesis. *Iskwew* is our word for woman. The *-sis* suffix denotes little. Directly translated, iskwesis means "little woman." So, like all words, it has power, it contains the history of our people. That word tells us how to treat little girls. We should treat them like little women. We should treat them like humans.

Beyond linguistics, beyond relationships between words, iskwesis contains the story of our people, of all the powerful women who came before us, our governance systems, our relationship to this land, our mothers. Everything about who you are and who you might become was contained in that single word your grandmother whispered in your ear.

Every word can be a complete story, can heal or can kill, so we have to be careful of the words we choose. Consider the word *illegal.* To say that something is illegal gives its status a fixed, final legitimacy—it says the status is natural, normal, and necessary. It's illegal, which means it's against the law, so it must be wrong. But to say it was *illegalized* denotes the status was conferred. It tells us that someone did that, gave it that status. At some point, someone decided it was not natural, normal, or necessary. Then we have to ask why.

There is a long story here. Alcohol is far more harmful than heroin or cocaine: its use is much more widespread. But because it is the recreational substance of choice for kiciwamanawak, it is legal. Heroin was perceived as a Black person's drug and was made illegal. Early in the twentieth century, as part of their campaign to illegalize it, opponents of cannabis started to call it marijuana for similar reasons. The story the new name told was that it was a drug for non-white people. In the twenty-first century, Canada changed the law about cannabis because too many kiciwamanawak boys ended up in prison and received socially debilitating criminal records. When we change the word to describe what really happened—in this case we added four letters to it, *-ized*—we remember the story is made up, and now it can be changed because it turns out that the story is bad for kiciwamanawak boys. Cannabis hasn't changed, the story we tell about it has. Word choice matters.

Every story is either a placebo or a nocebo, with the power to heal or to kill. We have to be careful of every single word we speak so that we do no harm. A single word can hurt or heal, and we have no way of knowing the result. Even a word intended as jest can wound. We never know how our words will be taken.

Now you know why knowledge keepers are so quiet, so careful with what they say. Our ancestors were known as great orators. Commissioner Morris was impressed by our ability to speak. But we were not long-winded. We knew the power of words and used them sparingly. We knew a war of words could take lives. Words can be weapons. Be careful with them.

Be very careful of everything you say. Every word that comes out of your mouth is a story. With every word you speak, every word you write, you can heal, or you can kill. So be careful. Watch what you say.

After you learn to be careful with what you say, then learn to be careful with what you hear—what you listen to. You become the stories you take in—the stories you inhale—the stories you believe.

There are some very powerful stories out there that we have to be careful of. The Canada story is a subchapter of the sovereignty story, and it's a very dangerous one. It includes the war story. In the mass-murder event that we refer to as the Second World War, over fifty million people were killed. People from this territory now called Canada participated in that mass murder. We tell ourselves a story about that event we call a war. We tell ourselves that our men died for our freedoms. It's a ridiculous story. Our freedom was never in jeopardy. But we continue to tell that story, and not just to ourselves: we tell it to our children. We have a special day set aside to tell that story. Every November 11, we bring out the story and retell it.

The Second World War had nothing to do with our freedom. It was merely the continuation of the mass murder event we call the First World War. The First World War was a continuation of hundreds of years of war between European nations. To them, war was a game, an adventure, a sport of sorts. The game got serious in the First World War, with machine guns and poison gas. The Second World War saw advancements in technology with airplanes and massive fire-bombing of civilians and, ultimately, nuclear weapons.

We should have learned.

We didn't.

We keep telling ourselves stories we know are not true, stories about the hero soldier, about the glory of war, about defending democracy.

I liked the Canada story of my youth. I joined the Canadian Armed Forces when I was seventeen. Back then the Canada story was about peacekeeping. We were part of the United Nations story. We were trying to do good in the world.

Then we sent soldiers to Afghanistan to kill brown-skinned people. We weren't peacekeeping. We weren't defending democracy. We weren't trying to make the world a better place. We joined with the United States in a revenge attack.

At the time it was hard to find out how many Afghani citizens were being murdered. We kept close count of the number of our soldiers that were killed, but it was bad publicity to mention how many civilians we murdered, so we didn't. We didn't include them in the war story. We didn't count their dead.

In retaliation for the attack on the World Trade Center, we participated in the murder of more than two hundred thousand Afghani people. Many of the dead were civilians who had nothing to do with al-Qaeda, or the Taliban, or even knew about the World Trade Center.

Instead, we told ourselves the story of the 158 Canadian soldiers who were killed in Afghanistan. We didn't talk much about the $18 billion we spent, the $2 billion to help rebuild the country after we had spent $16 billion destroying it.

We don't hear about Afghanistan much anymore. We don't want to hear the story. The country is in worse shape now than before we sent troops there, and it wasn't in great shape in the first place.

There are people inside the Canada story you hear, the one about prosperity and benevolent democracy and maple syrup, for whom it is a placebo story—and there are people outside the story. Many Aboriginal people don't feel they are part of the Canada story. Many of us feel it isn't ours. That's the reason we tend not to vote. It's not our election, it's not our government. We are outside of Canada, outside of its politics. This is a wealthy country. It's blessed with abundant natural resources. It is a place of prosperity, of opportunity, of promise. But not for us. We don't share in the wealth; we don't see opportunity. We don't belong in this story. We were written out. The story says we are victims, poor, helpless people on the fringes, dependent upon the benevolence of the dominant caste.

What happens when you're outside of the shared story? Did you know that 95 percent of men and 97 percent of women in prison were sexually or physically abused when they were children? I learned this from an Edmonton police officer who is working on his doctorate. Early on in their lifestory, these men and women were shown that they didn't matter. The message contained in their sexual and physical abuse was that they weren't worthy of the bigger story, the one about respect and freedom and belonging. The abuse story said that they were less than, that they didn't matter. The abuse story said they belonged to the victim story.

If they didn't belong in the big story, then the rules of that big story did not apply to them. They found belonging in alternate stories, the outsider stories, the story of gangs, of the outlaw, of the rebel, the reactionary, the substance use story. Nobody gave a shit about them. Why should they give a shit about Canada and its rules? It wasn't their story.

The victim story is a powerful nocebo story. Aboriginal people are told and tell themselves that they are the victims of colonization. Our subjugation, our suffering, persists and will persist as long as the colonization story is heard, told, repeated, and believed.

The victim story harshly impacts Aboriginal people. The story of our abuse at the hands of the colonizer is based in reality. Yes, we were sent to residential schools where we were abused, tortured, and even murdered. Yes, our people, especially our young men, are disproportionally incarcerated. Yes, our women and children are used to fill the jails. Yes, we have been dispossessed of our lands, forced into ghettos, and abandoned. The victimization has been real. Yet that is not the story that will save us.

Just like the difference between illegal and illegalized, *victim* is different than *victimized*. If you tell yourself a victim story, your lifestory is defined by that status: you are a victim. In the victimized story, something was done to you. It happened to you, but it is not who you are. You are still in charge of that. You can tell your own story.

Telling the victim story about Aboriginal people does not win sympathy or inspire change in the victimizers—the people who need to do the changing. It does not change government policy toward us. It does not change society's view of us. The more broadly the story is told, the more we are viewed as victims. The more we are viewed as victims, the more we are treated like victims. No one wants to hang out with losers.

The problem is—that's the way we have always been treated. The reason for residential schools and denigrating government policy is that we were viewed as victims of our own shortcomings—in need of civilization, in need of Christian salvation, in need of education, in need of domestication. As long as the rest of Canada and the world sees us as victims, if that's the story they tell themselves about us, that's the way we will be treated. Victims have no power of their own. They are dependent upon the largesse and charity of dominant society.

When I tell it that way, it sounds like the colonizers were trying to help us. In their minds they were. I don't know anyone who thinks of themselves as bad people. Even people who do bad things justify them by telling themselves a story about how what they are doing is the right thing to do in each circumstance. The man who beats up a woman is telling himself she deserves it, and that he is teaching her with his fists and his feet how to behave.

The problem with the victim story is not so much that it's told about us. Its ability to destroy comes from our telling the story to each other and to ourselves. When we are convinced we are victims—when we believe we are victims—we are trapped in a story where we will remain permanently as victims. The story won't let us out. When everyone tells the same story, when Canada and the world tell the Aboriginal victim story, when we tell it to ourselves, when everyone believes the story—the story will manifest itself and become reality.

The victim story is a nocebo story. It makes us sick. The more we hear it, the worse off we become. Our children are committing suicide because the victim story shows them no future and they have no hope. Our deplorable condition manifests itself in illnesses, in diabetes, in heart disease, in cancer. Our immune systems are weakened as much by the story of our victimhood as by our impoverished living conditions.

Victimhood is just one nocebo story. There are others—a lot of others. Listen to the news. In the current age, we have more of it than ever. All that constant broadcasting of negative stories has a health impact on the populace. Those stories that you watch about the murders and the violence—all the anger and the hate—those are all nocebo stories, and they are making you and everyone who consumes them sick. You don't even have to take a sugar pill. All you have to do is believe the story.

These are the stories we need to change as we prepare for a new era. We need stories of hope and possibility to nurture us. We need new heroes—environmental heroes, humanity heroes, and social development heroes.

We need to begin to tell ourselves placebo stories.

Placebo stories are not all in your mind. They are in your body. Your body actually gets better from the placebo effect. That is the power of story. Stories can heal you or they can kill you. They don't just heal or kill your mind with your choice of which stories you listen to, which stories you tell yourself. Stories can heal or destroy your body. You can cripple yourself with nocebo stories. The placebo effect isn't just thinking you feel better: your health genuinely improves. Your immune system is stronger, better able to fight off infections. Your internal organs work more optimally. Improved mental health improves physical health.

This is what I am trying to get across to you—the power of story.

You have to understand story in its full power before we get to the important parts.

When you first understand the power of story, you may feel like it's too late—that you can't change something so interwoven and embedded in the structure of our society. Yes, a lot of bad shit has already happened. But no, it's not too late to change the story. It's not fixed. You can edit a story after it's told. You can go back and make changes, important, relevant changes. That's what editing is. When we edit a manuscript, we go back through the story and retell it using different words, better words. You can edit your lifestory the same way. It's not so much what happened to you as what you tell yourself about it.

I took a severe beating when I was a child. For a while I told myself that I had been physically abused. I was sexually assaulted when I was ten. For a while I told myself that I had been sexually abused. I told myself victim stories. They diminished me. They made me weak and pathetic. I tried to overcome my weakness with anger and frequently spoke with my fists, until I started to become someone I did not like.

Then I retold myself those stories in a different way. I told myself a story of survival, of resilience. I quit hating my abuser. Now I pity him. My pity took his strength away from him.

All stories can be told in multiple ways. We can choose which version we want to tell ourselves. That's editing. We go back over our lifestory and rewrite it. We retell it in new, better ways, healing ways. And like editing a manuscript, we can edit the story many times, as many times as we want, because what we want out of our lifestory is a masterpiece.

Okay, then, if you think you have this, let's carry on.

Let me tell you about the snake.

I was given a powerful story about snakes. I really liked it. You know how some stories can make your skin crawl? Well, this snake story would make you want to tear your skin off, throw it in a pile, and run—that's how good it was.

The Canadian Challenge Dog Sled Race runs through here in the winter. This is one of the checkstops for that long-distance dog race. The mushers have a mandatory five-hour break here to rest their teams. It's great. We get to host really nice people and their hard-working, determined dogs. Well, this one year, there was a young woman who came through. I knew that after her five-hour rest she would leave at about sundown and would be mushing in the dark, so I was telling her scary stories. Just little things that happened around here over the years—spooky stuff.

I thought about telling her my snake story, and something told me to be careful. It was just a sense. We have a teaching about traditional stories that says we shouldn't tell them in the summer because telling certain stories can cause the snakes to come. But I looked around—there was three feet of snow on the ground—it was twenty below—it was the middle of February. I thought, it must be safe to tell my story—so I did.

The young woman left just before sunset. Her team looked strong as they sped out of the yard.

I like going to the Canadian Challenge Awards Breakfast held in La Ronge after the race is over. They serve a nice meal, and I get to visit with all my friends who took part in the race. The mushers get up to get their awards and prize money, and they often tell something about what happened to them on the trail. I like their stories.

Well, this young woman gets up and she tells about when she was leaving Johnson's camp, and, all of a sudden, all her dogs turned and looked into the forest. She said she looked, too, and there was something spooky there. So, she and her team got out of there as quickly as they could.

I felt a little proud of myself. I had scared her. My conceit in my storytelling ability put a smile on my face.

When I got back here, still grinning, my wife, Joan, was cleaning up where the dogs had been bedded down. Over there beside the cabin, see that slough? In the winter when it's frozen and covered with snow, you can park a half dozen dog teams there. I went to see if she had left anything for me to do. I met her on the trail and she said, "Did you see the snake?"

I said, "No, what snake?"

You have to know, when I met Joan, I promised her where we were going to live there were no wood ticks and there were no snakes, and here she was asking if I had seen the snake.

She said, "Yeah, at first I thought it was a bungie cord" as she kicked aside straw the dogs had used for bedding. And there it was, about eighteen inches or fifty centimetres long—green with a yellow stripe down its side—lying on the snow.

I haven't told that snake story since.

No. I am not going to tell it to you now.

That's the whole point of all this. I am trying to show you the power of story. If you tell a snake story, even in the middle of winter, when there is three feet of snow on the ground and it's twenty below, snakes can manifest themselves. Stories are powerful, and we have to be careful with them.

No. I am not telling the snake story, or any version of the snake story, or any other sacred story. Stories can heal and stories can kill. The snake story is about killing and revenge. If I give it to you and you use it carelessly, you might hurt yourself or someone else.

You can go to a knowledge keeper, and they might tell you a sacred story if you ask them for help. The story is the medicine. If you play with it, if you use it frivolously, if you try to publish it and make money from it, you could harm people. That's why knowledge keepers are careful with who they tell these stories to. It's not about secrecy or guarding knowledge. We don't tell these stories to just anyone who wants to listen to stories because of the damage that might result if they are used improperly.

Yeah, if you could get some more wood, that would be great. There's lots in the woodshed beside the cabin. It's starting to get darker now, and a bright fire will help.

I don't want to rank stories and say this one type is more important than those other types. All stories are important. All stories have power. But the story that is closest to you is your lifestory. It's the one you create, the one you tell yourself about yourself. It's your most immediate. It tells you and the world who you are.

Be careful with who you tell your lifestory to. Be careful how you tell it. I'm not telling you to keep your lifestory a secret. All I'm saying is take care. It's your story: guard it, take care of it, protect it. You are going to need it. Your personal story is a sacred story. It has power. It can change the world.

Your lifestory needs characters other than yourself. No story has only one character. Even the story of the person stranded on an island has the island and the water as supporting characters. You were born into a family. Those characters were chosen for you. But you get to choose if you are going to keep them in the story. You get to choose all the characters in your story. If the people you surround yourself with pull you down, endanger you, or bring disrespect—you can write them out of your story. Yes, it's that simple. If the people you surround yourself with are not the characters you want in your story, leave. Go somewhere else, find new, better characters. It's your story. You choose. Just remember: no matter where you go, there you are.

Be careful of the characters in your story. Treat them well.

When I was writing *Charlie Muskrat*, I started out with an idea that I wanted Wisahkicahk, the Trickster, to go to Mount Olympus and talk to the Greek gods. I created a character for Wisahkicahk to talk about— Charlie Muskrat. By page twenty-seven, the Mount Olympus conversation was done, and I still had an entire novel to write. Charlie took over.

My routine was to get up early on weekend mornings and write for a few hours. When my wife woke up later and was settled with her cup of tea, I would read to her what I had written that morning. That reading was the first edit.

It was like I had channelled Charlie. He became my friend. When I let him have his way, he took me and the novel in all sorts of unexpected directions. There were many mornings when I told Joan, "You are not going to believe what happened today!"

I learned that when we write, if we love our characters and treat them with respect, allowing them the freedom to become the best they can be, those characters become our best. They can exceed our expectations. Charlie Muskrat became my friend. By the end of the novel, he was very dear to me.

We can apply character development in fiction writing to how we treat characters in our lifestories. The life you are living is a story no different than the story you are writing. The only difference is one is relatively simple, while the other is complex—but the same principles apply. Don't have so many characters that the story becomes too complicated. Keep a few carefully chosen ones. Love them—treat them well and allow their story to unfold alongside yours.

Now keep in mind, as you select characters to accompany you in your lifestory, that you are also a character in their story. This is fundamental—you really need to pay attention to this part. Not everyone who creates their story treats their supporting characters well. Some writers are cruel to their characters.

Victims are characters in someone else's story that are treated badly. That's the very definition of victim—a character in a story not their own. Don't let others write you into a bad place. Even the fictional Charlie Muskrat was able to determine the path of the novel we wrote together. So can you.

There are many parallels between writing fiction and writing your own lifestory. It's very important which voice the story is told in. If you choose to tell the story in the third person—"She came to Harold Johnson to learn about stories"—then someone else is telling the story, not you. Third-person writing is the story of fate. People who believe in fate don't understand the power of telling their own story. It's not theirs. God is writing it. The devil is writing it. The forces of nature, the fictional forces of the market, the whole world, everybody else, is writing their story.

So, when you write your lifestory, make sure it is you who tells it. Tell it in the first person: "I went to Harold Johnson to learn about story." Then you are in control, you are telling your story. You are not a victim of fate. You are not being controlled and directed. Your life has not been predetermined. It's your story. You tell it.

I told you when I wrote Charlie Muskrat that I started with an idea and let it unfold. I started at the beginning and wrote to the end. Now, you might think that's the natural way to tell your lifestory. It isn't.

My friend Robert J. Sawyer once told me that he never starts to write a book unless he knows the ending. That was the opposite of the way I had been writing. I started with an idea and found the ending as I wrote. More often, I wrote until I was tired of the story and slapped an ending on it. That's not a good strategy. Sometimes the endings were unsatisfactory. I told myself that endings were hard to write. I told myself that I needed to get better at writing endings. I made lots of excuses for myself. But Robert was right. The best strategy is to know the ending and write toward it.

No, you don't know the details of the end of your lifestory. None of us knows the date, time, or circumstances. But we all know there is an end, and the end of your lifestory is just as important as the end of a fiction. It's a good strategy to be writing toward it all the time.

It's that last minute that's important. That moment when you know this is your last breath, your last heartbeat, your last thought. In that moment, you will be alone. None of the ancillary characters matter anymore. They might be there. Your family might be surrounding you as you lay dying in your own home. You might be in the hospital, or lying on the side of the road. You might have a medical professional assisting you to die. But that last moment will be yours alone.

This is the moment that will define your life.

The last line.

This is what the entire story you are creating has built toward. If in this moment you have regrets, it's your own fault. You were the author. But if in that defining moment you look back and say, "I am satisfied," then you have written a masterpiece.

As we author our lifestories, we have to keep that moment in mind. We need to keep contemplating our own mortality. It shouldn't fill us with fear or dread. It should instead feed us, motivate us, and give us strength.

When we accept our mortality, make peace with it, when death is our friend, then we truly understand the phrase, "Today is a good day to die." What we understand is that the phrase is not about dying. It's about the day. Today is a good day. It's such a good day that I am prepared to die. Every one of our days should be good enough to die in. It takes an incredible author to write days that good. We have to practise writing those days until we can fill our lifestory with pages so good that endings don't frighten us anymore.

When you are writing your lifestory, remember that your story shapes your reality. Edgar Allan Poe once wrote, "Believe nothing you hear, and only one half that you see." There is scientific evidence supporting the latter part of this quote. A lot of what we think we see simply isn't there. We have two eyes. We should see two pictures, one for each eye. Each of those pictures should be clear toward the centre and blurry around the periphery because most of the cones and rods, the things in our eyes that do the actual seeing, are clustered near the centre. Each of those two pictures should have a black hole in the middle because we cannot see through the optic nerve that occupies the centre of our retina.

What our brain does is take those two pictures and merge them. Then it fills in the blank spot. Do you know what our brain fills that blank spot in with?

Shit we make up.

The stories we tell ourselves are so powerful they can shape our perception of reality. When you look up at a starry sky, your brain will put stars in places where there are none. When you drop something small onto a patterned floor, your brain will maintain the pattern and hide the object you are looking for.

As an author I know to let someone else proof-read my work because if I intended to write *an* but inadvertently wrote *on*, when I reread the section my brain will show me *an* instead of what is actually on the page. Sometimes our brains lie to us—show us things that are not there.

You know there are horrible stories told about us. I'm sure you've heard them: the lazy, dirty, drunken Indian stories. These stories are powerful and damaging, not because they tell them about us, but because we hear them and we've heard them so often, for so long, that sometimes we take these ugly stories into ourselves and believe them. We make them part of our lifestory.

Racism is one of those ugly stories that gets passed along. It isn't a choice. We don't get rid of racism by attacking the racist. He doesn't believe he is racist. He believes the stories: Black people are not intelligent, Indians are drunks, Mexicans are violent, Arabs are terrorists, Chinese are good at math, white people are innocent. Racism is the story we tell ourselves and each other about race. If you believe any story about race, regardless of whether it is a good story or a bad one—you are a racist. Racism is nothing but story— pure story—no matter who tells it.

Struck a nerve, did I?

You don't like being told you are a racist.

Would it help you if I admitted I, too, am a racist?

Another story—this one about coffee. I like coffee. I like strong coffee. When I'm on the road, I know the best coffee is McDonald's. I was in a McDonald's, where I had just ordered four shots of espresso. It's a strange order, and it was taking time to fill. While I waited patiently, an Aboriginal woman walked in. She saw me—I assume she saw my braids—and came toward me. As she walked across that open bit of floor, I thought, Oh shit, here it comes. She's drunk and she's going to tell me about a sick relative and want twenty bucks to help her get back to the reserve. But then I had a second thought. I thought, No matter what, you treat this woman with respect.

When she came up, she just wanted to visit. To her, I was a friendly face in the crowd. I checked her out. Her shoes were new—so was her blouse. Her pants had a crease running down the front. Her hair was so clean it shone. I checked her breath: there was no alcohol or anything to cover up the smell. But that was not what my eyes had showed me in the first instant. My eyes lied to me. They showed me a dirty drunk where there was none.

So, anyone who says they are not a racist is full of shit if they are not checking their story every time. Because I have to, and I had a brown-skinned mother who loved me.

I am as much a product of story as everyone else. I cannot be otherwise, whether I want to be or not. Story encompasses the parameters of my consciousness, of my existence, of my very being. It tells me who I am, where I came from, and where I belong.

I am story.

I have contemplated abdicating my race—writing myself out of the race story. I know that the genetic difference between the various races is extremely minor. We share 99.9 percent of our DNA with each other. The variations between two people of the same race can be greater than the variation between either of them and a person from a different race. Biologically, we are all the same, with the only difference being skin, eye, and hair colours that are attributable to various climates. Underneath those different colours, we are all humans, *Homo sapiens.* We all originated in Africa, and some of us lost our blackness during our migrations northward.

I don't define myself racially. I am Cree and Swede. Those are cultural terms, not biological distinctions. Growing up, I wasn't influenced by my father's Swedish culture. He came here and assimilated into the Aboriginal community. He became a trapper and a fisher.

My mother's Cree culture did have a huge impact on me. Here I find the definition of myself. I have grown up and lived immersed in Cree culture. It has been all around me all my life. It's in my preference for wild food, in my sense of humour, in the way I relate to people and to the environment. Cree culture has shaped my identity.

Even though culture and race are completely different things, they are usually not perceived that way in our shared stories. Cultural variations are often attributed to racial categories, frequently in negative and false stories: Black people are violent, Aboriginals are lazy, people from the Middle East are extremists.

It would be easy to abdicate my race. It's only a minor biological difference without any real significance. The problem is that I would be expected to also abdicate my culture. Kiciwamanawak tend to believe that they do not have a race. To them race is a category for other people. They also tend to not believe that they have a culture, even though, or maybe because, theirs is the dominant one. So, if I were to publicly abdicate my race, it would likely be taken that I had abdicated my culture at the same time, which would make me cultureless. And if I were to be cultureless, then those kiciwamanawak who believe they are without culture would think that I had become like them. Then, more horribly, they would insist that everyone do like Harold Johnson and abdicate their race so that we could all live together as one big family, everyone the same, meaning everyone like them, without race or culture, meaning with their race and culture, and the assimilation project would be complete.

I know you have culture. But culture is made up of all the stories we tell ourselves, and the problem, as we've seen, is that we sometimes take everything that's going on around us as natural. If all the people in your community are doing things exactly the same way you do things, pretty soon you start to think that's the right way to do things and it would be best if everyone were to do things this way.

It's okay. We all do it. We get to believing that our way is the natural and normal way, the way everyone should follow, and forget that other people might do things differently.

A very common story kiciwamanawak tell themselves about their culture is that they are innocent. It's not their fault. They didn't do anything. Historical crimes, residential schools, and the sixties scoop, which is still going on, were not their fault. They tell themselves that they are being unfairly punished for things they did not do—that they are innocent victims. When you are innocent and a victim, the world looks scary. It seems everyone is out to get you. That story, that your race is being treated unfairly, is also a racist story. Anyone who believes that story, who tells it to themselves and to others, is a racist. It's that simple.

Your race has nothing to do with who you are.

Our culture, the stories we tell each other about who we are, where we came from, and where we belong, that is what's important. The quantum of Indigenous blood required to qualify for a government issued status card is not important. The card symbolizes that the government—the dominant culture—recognizes us, but the government cannot tell us who we are.

I recently met a flat-Earther. It surprised me. The young man seemed otherwise reasonably intelligent, and we were having a gentle conversation when he scoffed at the concept of a spherical planet. This isn't new. There were conspiracy theories before the internet. People doubted the moon landings. We've probably had a small population of people who consistently believed the earth was flat since long before Christopher Columbus.

The experience made me wonder—why would someone with information readily available choose to believe the Earth is flat? I started to ask questions. I was curious. Then it came to me—he didn't believe the dominant stories because he had already learned that many of them were false. The young man was Aboriginal. He'd been told lies all his life about himself and the people he originated from. When we discover that someone has lied to us, we tend not to believe anything further that person has to say. The same seems true for society. When a story society tells us turns out to not be true, some of us will distrust everything society tells us.

We all need stories to help us make sense of things. When people don't believe one set of stories, they adopt a different set of stories. Then they find people who share the alternative story, and they become a community. Communities are held together by the stories they tell each other. When everyone in the community is telling and believing the same story, the perceived truth of that story increases. It becomes their reality.

The conspiracy theorists are right. I give them credit. The stories dominant society tells us are not true—because there are no true stories. All the stories we tell ourselves are made up. The conspiracy theorists recognize this and are a little ahead of most people in greater society who believe the bulk of society's stories. Where the conspiracy theorists fall short is that they create other stories to replace the dominant stories and believe the new stories as true. It's this belief that there is such a thing as an absolutely true, unchangeable story that leads them astray.

Now most of you are nodding your heads, thinking, "Yes, yes, those flat-Earth people have it all wrong." But what I am trying to convince you of is that we, too, have it all wrong.

Stories evolve. Dominant culture—that is to say the culture that transformed from hunter-gatherer to agrarian societies about ten thousand years ago, then transformed again during the Industrial Revolution, and now finds itself in the midst of an information revolution—has told itself a consistently evolving story.

The story is that there is such a thing as truth and there are absolute truths. The beginning story of this society was the religion story with an infallible all-knowing God who encapsulated absolute truth. Those who had remained hunter-gatherers, like my people, didn't need that story. We understand the world around us as being in a constant state of flux and change, ephemeral and shape-shifting. The concept of truth, that there is one absolute way of knowing that never changes, doesn't assist in understanding our environment, and doesn't allow for adaptation to the constant change inherent in that environment.

But if you want a society that stays in one place and grows crops and builds villages, then towns, then stone-walled cities, you need a story of permanence. You need to believe that things will always stay the same. To do that, you create a fiction called truth. Truth is simply an idea that we give meaning to. It doesn't exist in nature. A tree grows, it dies and falls down, bugs eat it, it becomes soil that feeds a new tree. Where is the truth in that? There isn't any because the concept isn't needed. None of the other species on this planet we share need truth as part of their existence. Only the *Homo sapiens* species tells itself that a made-up concept called truth is important. But really there are no true stories, because truth itself is a story.

When dominant society adopted religion and the concept of truth as a way of staying together, that story held for ten thousand years, growing more and more complex as it evolved. But it always kept the same fundamental basis that there was something called *truth* and only those who followed the faith knew that truth.

Francis Bacon, the creator of the scientific method, believed in truth. He was firstly a devout Christian. Science is now seen as the alternative to religion, but its fundamental principles remain a search for truth and hence a search for God. Even Einstein once said, "The more I study science, the more I believe in God." Science might seem anti-religion, but its founding principles are born out of religious dogma, that elusive search for truth.

When quantum physicists began to see the impermanence of matter, they had trouble understanding what they were observing. That a thing could be and not be at the same time confused them. They had no stories to help them makes sense of it. All of the stories told in their society taught them that things either were or were not, truth or untruth. Several of them came to Aboriginal Peoples and asked for guidance. We understood. We had stories. We knew about those things the scientists were discovering. It was Aboriginal knowledge, encompassed in Aboriginal language, that helped present-day quantum physicists understand what they were observing.

To understand the inner workings of the atom, you have to abandon concepts of real and not real, here and not here. Subatomic particles are everywhere and nowhere at the same time. The old concepts of truth and permanence, for ever and ever amen, are distractions that get in the way of this understanding.

Quantum physicists might have moved on from religious stories to find meaning, but the rest of dominant society has not. Academia's roots are in religious orders. The university was first a theological institution. There, too, the fundamental belief in the concept of truth persists. Academics fundamentally believe they know something real, something true, that their research and their theories are quests for truth.

I need a bit of a break. All this talking is giving me a dry throat.

Man, this tea is nice even when it's cold. I think it must be the mint that's so soothing. There's lots there if anyone else wants some. Hot tea, anyone? Hot tea on a cool evening.

I cannot tell you who you are. That's for you to decide.

I can tell you where to go look for the answers—where to find out who you are, where you came from, and where you belong—but I cannot tell you who you are. You have to find that for yourself. This isn't bad news. This is good news. I am telling you to go on a journey, to explore and discover, to experience and live, and to author the best story possible for yourself.

I'll give you some hints about where I go to find my story.

In 1995 a man named Victor Gorshkov published a book called *Physical and Biological Bases of Life Stability: Man, Biota, Environment.* In it he explains his research into the information that flows through the Earth's biota. He concluded that to replicate that amount of information with modern computers would require a computer the same size as all the Earth's biota, and all that would be achieved by attempting the replication would be the change from a carbon system to a silicone system.

Think about that for a moment.

Think about all the information flowing through the boreal forest here where we live. Not just up and down the trunk of the tree from roots to leaves. Information flows through the mycelia between the trees, carrying messages, and transporting nutrients. And not just the plants, the shrubs, and bushes; the biota includes the microbes, and the bacteria, the fungi and lichens and mosses. The soil itself is a living, breathing entity. The biota includes the animals, the squirrels and the deer and the elk and the birds and the fish.

All the information in constant flow throughout our forest is story. It is story in action. I have been trying to tell you how powerful stories are, and this is my best explanation. If you can grasp this concept, imagine all that power. Imagine story so strong it shapes life itself. Imagine story as a dynamic force embedded in everything. I take Gorshkov's ideas even further. The story that flows through the Earth's biota is not confined to those parts that we consider living. The rocks, too, are in the story. So is the water. Those lakes and rivers and streams are part of that powerful story.

Now let's start putting things together for you.

I told you that the Christian God was story. Their bible states, "In the beginning was the word and the word was with God and the word was God." Now imagine all that information flowing through the Earth's biota, that powerful dynamic story. Can you imagine God in there? If you can, then imagine the information flows through the universe—imagine those vast webs of energy that look like mycelia that scientists are seeing when they look out into the far distant sky. Can you imagine that amount of information, the complexity of that dynamic story, all those words. Probably not. It's okay if you can't. God is supposed to be incomprehensible.

Remember what I told you about our ancestor's atoms in the soil, how the plants reach down and bring those atoms to the surface and animals eat those plants and we pick the berries off those plants and eat the animals that eat the plants and so we have our ancestors' atoms in us. That, too, is part of the story.

In Cree when we finish praying, we say "kakithaw nawakomakanak." It means "all my relations." Not just my biological relations. I am also related to the plants and animals here. They contain my ancestors' atoms. I am related to the sky and the water. I am related to the fish and the birds and the worms. I am related to the spirit forces here. I call the Great Spirit Grandfather, and I call the Earth Grandmother.

Now remember who we are. Residential schools erased our language. Our ceremonies were banned, churches proliferated—further destroying our understanding of ourselves and our place on this planet. Government policy kept us confined to our tiny reserves. Greenpeace attacked the fur trade to the point that it isn't worth going out anymore.

Welfare was forced on the people. My mother was told that she had to quit trapping and fishing because she was taking us out of school to go with her on the spring muskrat hunt. She was a widow with six children at home and in the mid-1960s was earning five to eight hundred dollars a day during the trapping season. She embarrassed the men. When the government found out she was taking us out of school, they told her she had to move to La Ronge and go on welfare or they would take her children away. In 1967, if you told an Aboriginal woman that you were going to take her children away, she would do whatever you said, because at that time they were taking Aboriginal women's children away.

We weren't the only ones whose only option was welfare.

I was fortunate. I was taken out to the trapline and taught how to live on the land. Mom moved to La Ronge and went on welfare, but she still took me to the trapline with her in the spring. I had that experience to carry me through my life. Many of our people did not. It only takes one generation to remove the knowledge. If Mom or Dad stops trapping, the children don't learn, and the next generation, the grandchildren, have no knowledge of living on the land. Two generations later and we have the dysfunction that characterizes our communities. Then imagine the generations that have moved to urban centres. They have no connection to the land, to the powerful sustaining story, to their ancestors' atoms.

So, you—you want to know who you are. Like I said, I can't tell you that. You have to find out for yourself. Go out to the forest, connect with the trees, with the water, with the animals. That's where the story of our people exists. Learn those stories. Use them to make connections. That's who you are.

We're in a good era now. Land-based healing and land-based education are being recognized as superior ways of doing things.

What if you are Indigenous and you grew up in a city? I don't think you are missing out because you haven't exercised your rights recently. Our ancestors

who negotiated the treaties knew what was important. That's why they insisted on keeping the right to
hunt, fish, trap, and gather. They knew that connection to the land was our identity. Without it, we would
be nobody. In every one of the numbered treaties we
negotiated, our ancestors insisted upon those land
rights. We only agreed to treaty when we were promised that the government would not interfere in our
way of life, that the reserves were there for when we
wanted to settle down. Commissioner Morris, who
negotiated on behalf of the Crown, promised that
we could live as before and everything granted in the
treaties, the horses and plows and five dollars a year,
was on top of what we already had.

When they negotiated an adhesion to Treaty Six in
this territory, my great-grandfather James Ross was
there. He came away with the understanding that he
could continue to live anywhere he wanted in this territory. He never moved to the reserve—always lived
out on the land—built a cabin wherever he wanted—
stayed the winter. In the summer he travelled around,
living in a tent. When he and my great-grandmother
were old, when he couldn't go out hunting so much,
they lived primarily on rabbits they caught in their
snares. They never owned much. By Western standards they were poor. But I am sure that when they

got to that last moment of their lives, as they were taking that last breath, that they were satisfied. They had lived a complete story.

Today there are only very few of us still on the land. Most either live on reserves or have migrated to urban centres. Hunting, fishing, trapping, and gathering are carried on by a tiny minority. We've lost our way. We don't know who we are anymore. We've lost our identity and our place.

In 1930, the government of this province assumed authority over the natural resources in this territory. The Natural Resource Transfer Agreement negotiated between Saskatchewan and the federal government stipulated that the province would have the right to regulate our hunting in order to preserve game. To me that is bizarre. We had managed the resources here for millennia and always had enough. In a few quick years, kiciwamanawak had destroyed the buffalo. Yet they believed they were better suited to look after hunting rules.

The NRTA is a constitutional document. It is one of the founding documents this country is built upon. It purports to protect our rights to hunt and fish and gather—at the same time that it takes away our right to manage the resources. It takes away the right to live as before that Commissioner Morris assured us of. The

132 HAROLD R. JOHNSON

continued freedom we were promised vanished with the government of Canada's transference of control over the resources in this territory to the provincial government.

Here in the North, it's not so bad. We still have space to go hunting. Our relatives in the southern part of the province are not so fortunate. In Treaty Four territory, the vast majority of the land has been taken up for farming. The right to hunt, fish, trap, and gather is meaningless if you have no space to exercise that right.

I'm just going to take a break here for a moment, get up and stretch my legs. When I get back, I'm going to talk about that lazy, dirty, drunken Indian story.

A friend of mine gave me a book by Alan Fry, *How a People Die*. He wanted to know my opinion of it.

Fry was an Indian agent, writing in 1970. He tried to sound empathetic. He tried to appear understanding. His conclusion that Indians are just so different from white folks that many will not survive in the modern era is derived from the limits of his understanding. He observed this from within a deeply ingrained ideology that would not allow him to imagine beyond its narrow confines. The story of him and his people was so natural to him that he could not think outside of it, and all of his interpretations, all of his inferences, were shaped by that overarching story.

It was a hard read for me when he talked about the filthy houses where children were neglected, where alcohol created the equivalent of opium dens of squalor and hopelessness. He tried to sound fair, and I am sure that in his mind he was being compassionate and considerate.

He writes about failed alcohol policy that allowed Indians into bars and prevented off-site sale, which meant they would drink as much beer as they could pour into their bellies before the bars closed. Throughout, he offers solutions to the problem of people who are able to work but refuse to, people who have become dependent on welfare and alcohol.

The book is small and so is his thinking.

His stories contradict the stories I know. He talks about kind logging operators who willingly hired Indians only to have the Indians work for a short time then quit. My stories are about our people going to work cutting fenceposts for the post man only to be not paid, and stories about Indians being brought to work and paid in whiskey.

I survived the logging camps in the late seventies and early eighties, but I was white-passing and prepared to fight back. The racism in the logging and mining camps was blatant. The darker skinned you were, the more likely you were to be assigned lackey work—the work that dignified white people wouldn't stoop to perform.

What Fry misses is a hundred years of the Indian Act prior to his appointment as an Indian agent. His version of the residential school was that these were good places where children whose parents could not look after them properly were sent. He laments that the government was put to the expense of taking the children away.

Fry is a great apologist for Indian Affairs. He decries the unfair treatment of Indian agents. To him, the Indian agent is the last hope for Indians, maligned and criticized for everything they do and don't do. In his mind, everyone in the department was working as hard as they could to help the Indians. To him, the problem was the people didn't understand budgetary constraints.

Fry confirms all of the stereotypes: Indians are given too much welfare and it has made them lazy and dependent. They are given free houses that they destroy. They are genetically inferior and prone to alcohol abuse. They cannot be helped because they don't want help. They want to live in squalor and filth, and Darwinism is going to kill off those unfit or unable to adapt to modern white society.

I've known several people like Fry, white men who came to the North because promotions and career advancements were easier here. After they had reaped all of the benefits of a good government job administering us, they went back south and proclaimed themselves experts on the Indian problem.

The problem with Fry's work is that he hits on all stories that underlie the contemporary racist narrative about us. It's a retelling of the lazy, dirty drunk story. He tells it as the expert, hands on, on the front line, immersed in the filth and stink and hopelessness.

But he isn't immersed. He's never part of the community. He views us through the lens of the outsider, through the eyes of the expert, from his superior white background. He is too far removed from nature. To him the best thing for the Indian is to work in the logging camps, deforesting and erasing their heritage. What he laments is that we do not adopt his story, adopt his values. Because he views us as inferior people in need of his salvation, he never learns about our stories, our connections, the stories about when we were beautiful human beings.

Fry starts out with a description of filthy, drunken squalor. He tells of people caught in hopeless, despotic misery, living in houses of disrepair and neglect, that he as an Indian agent cannot effect change because the people inhabiting the houses won't change. The hard part about reading his version is that I remember the shacks. Our community was not on reserve, we did not have Indian Affairs housing. People put together what they could with what they had. Some of my school friends lived in those shacks, and so did some of my cousins. Later, when I moved around northern communities, I occasionally found those same shacks. In the eighties, I sometimes partied in those shacks.

In the hundred years of the Indian Act that Fry misses are the roots of the despair and hopelessness that he encountered. Residential schools had already traumatized huge swathes of the Indian population. In his view, our traditional beliefs and ways of being were no longer valid and did not serve us in the modern era. What he misses is that the government he worked for had been and remained very diligent in eradicating those beliefs and ways of being. Our ceremonies, the Sundance and the Potlatch, were outlawed. Our spiritual connection to the land was severed. Missionary zeal, assisted by direct government funding to the churches, had unleashed savage Christianity upon us for a century before the Indian Act.

Even before the Christians with their churches, diseases we had no immunity to decimated our population, and with that population loss, we lost many knowledge keepers, healers, thinkers, and leaders. This trauma preceded residential schools and impacted us at a population level. We were in grief when we negotiated the Numbered Treaties. That great wounding weakened us, so we had no resistance to the further traumas that awaited us under the Indian Act.

Trauma is real. We have only recently begun to understand it. We began to explore it as post-traumatic stress disorder after the Vietnam War. It is still understood only marginally and prescribed treatments are vastly inadequate. But to my mind, there is something underlying and preceding the trauma, something that first weakened us, so that we lost our immunity to grief and hurt and soul wounding. We lost our spiritual connection to the healing power of the land and water.

We talk lots about residential schools. But they and their concomitant trauma don't completely account for our present condition. An uncle of mine, who for many years lived in one of those alcohol dens and subjected his children, my cousins, to its horrors, never went to residential school. Neither did his parents. He never did learn to read and write. I knew him better in his later, more sober, years and witnessed him repair an engine that younger educated men couldn't. He figured out how to precisely install a timing belt on a modern automobile engine by looking at the pictures in a repair manual that had been left by one of the people who could read but couldn't get it right.

He was one of the best hunters I have ever known. His woods skills were superior to any today and even surpassed many of his own era. When he was on the land, he was in his element. It was only in town where he struggled to survive. This is not unusual. I know many people, myself included, who have fled back onto the land to recover. It seems here in Northern Saskatchewan if you say "land" and "healing" in the same sentence, you don't have to explain anymore. Many of us have at one time, or have a relative we know, who simply goes to the trapline when things are not going very well. For some, at least, it's a chance to get away from alcohol, away from communities that can devolve into cycles of intoxication.

I knew a family in a far northern community that also lived in one of those squalid alcohol dens in the 1970s that Fry was talking about. The sons of that family were sought by exploration and mining companies for their incredible skills and were famed for their hard, diligent work. Everyone knew that if you got one of those boys out into a bush camp, you couldn't ask for a better worker. But when they came back to town, when they were out of their element—they spent all their money on alcohol and sold anything they had to buy more.

There is a man I respect for his bush skills, who I learned some of my skills from, who told me that the people he respected in the bush were those sons from that family. He was very familiar with them, having grown up beside them. He told me that those men had built-in compasses in their heads and it was impossible for them to ever become lost. He recounted one time when an exploration crew got stranded and planes could not go get them due to heavy forest fire smoke that limited visibility. L (one of the sons) led that crew over a hundred miles cross-country, kept them fed along the way, and came out precisely at a mining camp that he had never been to before. He told me these men would leave their community in Northern Saskatchewan and travel cross-country, up into the barren lands in the Northwest Territories, guided primarily by instinct, and come out precisely where they intended at another community.

Over the years I have met a few others similar to them—people who had an innate sense of self and nature—people who thrived on the land and were purposeless in organized communities. We often met when I defended or prosecuted them for their drunken in-town misbehaviour. As defence counsel I often requested, and as a prosecutor I often suggested, that they be released if they agreed to go to their trapline and stay there until their pending trial. If they were out on the land, they were no bother to anyone.

A few years ago, a good friend of mine helped initiate and run a land-based healing program that incorporated Western trauma counselling. They had a success rate of over 70 percent. This is phenomenal. Most twenty-eight-day treatment programs for substance-use disorders only have success rates of between 2 and 5 percent: 2 percent if you go to a treatment centre for our people; 5 percent if you spend thousands of dollars per week and travel to a place like Vancouver.

I asked my friend what the hell he was doing. He said, "Harold, you won't believe it. Sometimes when I bring people back at the end of the day, they're crying. They say, 'I'm an Indian, but I never set a fishnet before. I'm an Indian, but I've never set a rabbit snare before.'"

Then I understood what he was doing. He was giving them back their identities—I am an Indian. He was giving them back a sense of belonging—I belong on the land. When you have an identity and sense of belonging, you can begin your healing journey.

It's not just going out on the land and doing traditional activities. My friend explained that the best results come when storytelling is added. When setting a fishnet, tell stories about setting nets, and the same with setting snares. Tell them how the old people used to do it. He said the storytelling component was just as important as the activity. When the people put the two together, hands-on experience in an inherent historical context, they came away with a much richer experience.

This connection to the land is far more than a mere emotional or intellectual attachment. It's not a simple preference. It's something far deeper than that. It is a spiritual connection. It's a connection to one's ancestors, a connection to the life forces, a connection to the Great Spirit and to Creation.

Kiciwamanawak lost their connection ten thousand years ago in the failed Agrarian Revolution. They, too, had been hunter-gatherers, but some of them chose to live in settlements and grow crops. Their lives were significantly worse than before. When they were hunter-gatherers and a food source did not provide one year, all the other food sources were still available. Now if their crops failed, they starved. People in settlements could not move to where the food was abundant and so they suffered accordingly. Agrarian societies organized themselves hierarchically. Those nearer to the pyramid pinnacle lived off the work of those nearer the base. Hierarchy introduced the concept of authority. Authority is completely foreign to hunter-gatherers.

The biggest problem with agrarian society was that once entered, it was impossible to go back, even after people recognized their new way of life was worse than the hunter-gatherer life they had forsaken. Large families, required for the intense labour involved in early agriculture, were too big to sustain with hunting and gathering. Those who usurped others' personal authority insisted upon maintaining their new positions of authority and so prevented a return. There was no going back, and they simply made the best of their miserable lives until their experience and memory erased all that had been before and they came to believe that their pitiful, hierarchical existence was natural, normal, and necessary. Kiciwamanawak has not had a spiritual connection to the land for over ten thousand years. They cannot be expected to understand.

The spiritual imperative "you are in charge" is powerful. It informs much of our original culture, including the principle of non-interference. If everyone in your society is in charge of their own lives and their own connection to the Great Spirit and to Creation, then no one has any business telling, or even suggesting, that anyone else do things differently.

We know that children—little people who recently arrived here from the spirit world—retain their connection to that realm and only slowly lose it as they grow. When a little person declares "You are not the boss of me," they are expressing the spiritual imperative that they are in charge of their lives. They should be encouraged. Instead, they are frequently introduced to the concept of parental authority. Sadly, in Western culture, that inborn understanding of self is often beaten out of the child.

Old people, as they near the ends of their lives, again get closer and closer to the spirit world from whence they came as they get ready to return to it. They re-experience the imperative "you are in charge," and begin to refuse to do as they are told by mere humans. This confuses their children and people assigned as caregivers, who view them as stubborn and uncooperative.

Please do not confuse what I am calling the spiritual imperative of "you are in charge" with the Christian concept of commandment. In our understanding, the Great Spirit demands nothing from us. Instead, we are furnished with guiding principles that will assist us in our journey through this physical world. We remember or forget them at our peril. These are definitely not laws. Law requires authority and is a symptom of a people who have lost their sense of self and became reliant upon systems. Law is required by people who have severed their spiritual connections. They no longer know how to be. They need someone to tell them. Those in their societies who have usurped others' personal authority fill this void. They are happy to tell people what to do.

Remember what I said about sovereignty, about how my ancestors' atoms in the soil and in the plants and animals and in me and my atoms returning to the soil connect me to this territory? It's more than that. It's more than a legal relationship with the land, more than a familial relationship. It's a powerful spiritual connection as well.

Imagine love so immense that a mere human is incapable of enduring it all. Imagine happiness, likewise, so intense that at its height it is hard to endure. Then add to this the experience of being a spirit in a physical body, knowing that the only person in charge of your life is yourself. You are whole and complete. You are plugged in to the neural networks, the mycelia, the root systems of the forest. You experience and can translate energy and frequencies. You are repeatedly told by the spirits of the plants and animals and insects, "you are a beautiful human being."

I would like to dispel a myth. We were not animist. We did not pray to the trees. We prayed *with* the trees. We recognized that trees were in a constant state of prayer, communicating between the earth and the sky, and we could join them. And not just trees. The animals pray, as do the water and the rocks. We can send our prayers with and through them, and the Great Spirit will hear us and answer. This communication between humans and the environment was further facilitated through the act of ceremony, the Sundance, the Sweat Lodge, where whole communities cooperate in the communication, where they send and receive messages.

In the state of nature, which John Locke decried as wasteful and ignorant, you quickly learn that you can have all that you want, the Great Spirit provides, and you live a pampered existence. You learn to not worry about tomorrow; the Great Spirit will provide. If what is given to you today is too much for your immediate needs, you share with your community. If you kill a moose and want to keep it, the best place to store it is in the belly of another hunter and in the bellies of his or her children. "You are in charge" doesn't mean that you are abandoned, alone and on your own. It means that you make the decisions and the spiritual forces that surround you will assist. They're your helpers. You decide where you want to go, and if you work with them, they will help you get there.

Then into paradise enters tragedy. First, diseases to which we have no immunity killed so many that the consciousness of whole peoples (sometimes mistakenly referred to as nations) was deeply wounded. Our recovery system, nature through ceremony, was illegalized: it was made illegal and so deemed unnatural, abnormal, unnecessary. Swarms of preachers descended upon us, telling anyone who would listen that if they went to the forest to pray, they were praying to Satan and would go to hell and burn forever. The Indian Act forced relocation onto tiny, cramped reservations, and all liberty and the right to make decisions were removed. Children were forced into residential schools where they were tortured and raped, and if they survived the spiritual, emotional, and physical neglect with its concomitant rampant diseases and sometimes deliberate murders, they returned to their communities deeply traumatized.

Traders brought whiskey.

If you once had a powerful spiritual connection that was severed by laws and priests and policies, it doesn't take away the need for that connection. The need remains unfulfilled. Alcohol cunningly promises to fill that need. It soothes the hurt. Intoxication feels a little bit like spiritual fulfillment. People emptied of spirit—by laws, by priests, by residential schools, by day schools, by welfare agents, by Indian agents, by colonial institutions, by deforestation and ecological ruin of their traditional territories—hunger to have their spirit filled. When they encounter alcohol, they pour it into their inner void.

It's a false promise. They do not find love and happiness so immense it is hard to endure. Instead, they find filth and squalor and pain and grief and even more trauma from the violence inherent in alcohol consumption. This time we are the bringers of trauma as we beat our wives and our children and each other. Death and violence and grief and trauma become normal. The distance between self and spiritual connections becomes even greater, and more alcohol is taken to try to fill the growing void.

There is another spiritual imperative. All my relations, which is commonly spoken at the end of prayers and ceremony, reminds us that we are related to all of the natural world: the Plant Nations, the Standing Nations of trees, the Animal Nations, those that swim, those that fly, and those that crawl, to the Sun and the Moon and the Water. We are also related to all the spirits between Earth and Heaven. This "all my relations" acknowledgement not only strengthens our connection to the land and to nature, it just as importantly strengthens our connections between us and our human relations.

We were a sharing society. We looked after each other. Today I don't see the level of sharing that I saw in my youth. Many of us have become affluent and it is among this population that sharing has diminished, probably because the achievement of affluence requires a stepping away from community. The poor among us still share, and it seems the poorest share the most. The people you see panhandling are prone to giving away almost as much as they are gifted. I know hunters today who still proudly feed the people, but there are fewer and fewer as we have lost our connection to the Great Spirit and the wonders that he provides.

The greatest diminishment of our people came about from the attack on our women. Western culture vastly undervalues the role of women and only recently has begun to allow them into their centres of governance. I am privileged to have been alive when women were still responsible for community cohesion.

The first schoolteacher in our community wrote in his journal in 1942 that the matriarch of Molanosa was Jeannie Ross. I do not have a clear memory of her, just an old woman walking down the road dressed in black, but I do remember the stories. She was a medicine woman, famed for her abilities not only in our community, but also in neighbour communities. Jeannie had six children and was never seen with a man. I'm not at all suggesting immaculate conception. She took a man when she needed one. She built her own cabins, her own canoe, had her own dog team, did her own hunting, fishing, and trapping. When we were researching the history of Aboriginal Peoples in Prince Albert National Park, we came across an entry that stated: "When Mrs. Ross is about to have a baby, she gets in her canoe and paddles away by herself." Jeannie's son William bragged that he was born under a spruce tree on the south shore of Montreal Lake.

When Jeannie died, our community transitioned to male leadership. The self-appointed new leader ingratiated himself to the colonial forces. He made sure he was friendly with the conservation officer, the schoolteacher, and any government official who might have reason to come to our community. The problem was that he only looked after his own extended family. He made sure they reaped the benefits of any services before anyone else. The other families could not, or would not, put forth their own leaders.

I know a woman who lived in Northern Manitoba who told me about when the government people came to negotiate a new hydro development in her home territory. They had sent word that they were coming, and when their plane landed, they were met by a delegation of women. Confused, they said they had come to negotiate with the community leaders and left. They were invited back and this time they were met by men and negotiations ensued. The only problem was the men could not make decisions and kept leaving the meeting to ask the women what they should say. The friend who told me this story was a young girl at the time.

When we started the Northern Alcohol Strategy, an Elder from La Ronge reached out to me. He said, "I need to talk to you." He told me that before 1965 there was some drinking in La Ronge, but it was a sometimes thing. Someone would get a case of beer or a gallon of wine and it would be shared around. That changed with the opening of the Anglo-Rouyn Mine north of town. The miners came to town and had a party on the reserve that went twenty-four hours a day, with night shift workers replaced by day shift workers, and the entire purpose was to get Aboriginal women drunk.

He said there was another party on the other side of town with the smoke jumpers, men who fought forest fires. They, too, only invited Aboriginal women. The

Elder told me that if a man went to either of those parties, there was usually a fight, so the men quit going.

He said there was another group of white men who came—rich American tourists. They flew in on private planes and did not bring their families. They, too, preyed on Aboriginal women and brought the hard liquor, whiskey, vodka, and rum.

If you want to destroy a people, attack the women first.

When a people have experienced a huge spiritual loss, when they have been disconnected from the land, when their governance system has been undermined, when their understanding of their role on the planet is completely at odds with modern society, they frequently experience a huge void in their being, an emptiness. Their inherent skills and abilities have no value in a rampant consumption society. They are made to feel worthless. They survive as best as they can.

They attempt to fill the void with substances that feel as though they might be medicine. Alcohol alleviates all of the symptoms of PTSD during the period of intoxication, so people frequently self-medicate with it. Alcohol might be called spirits, but it has no spiritual component to it. It is a pseudo-spirit, a false promise. It lies. But even worse, alcohol destroys what spirit remains. It doesn't fill the void, it enlarges it.

After a bout of drinking, people are left emptier than before, and that emptiness drives them back to the bottle for a refill.

I've been working hard to help Aboriginal Peoples change the story we tell ourselves about alcohol. I've seen successes before COVID. We can change the story at a community level. But with the pandemic and government insistence that alcohol is an essential good, I'm afraid those early successes have been reversed.

My reason for helping our people to sober up has an underlying purpose. Sobriety is just the first step. There is a prophecy I have known about for decades that tells us, "Hard times are coming. Get ready. As Aboriginal people you don't have much to worry about, but the white people are really going to suffer. They are going to come and ask us how to live on this planet." It's that prophecy—and now I see it coming true with COVID, and undeniable climate change—that motivates me. We are never going back to the way it was before, and the hardships we now experience are going to continue to worsen. If the prophecy continues to be correct and it's our role to help kiciwaman-awak, our cousins, live on this planet, then we have to sober up and remember in time. We might experience huge spiritual voids that we want to fill, but kiciwamanawak don't even know that they are empty and need to reconnect with the land to fill the need they are trying to fill with consumerism. They, too, feel a driving need, but in the story of their society, they are told the need will be satisfied with more stuff, more televisions, bigger trucks, nicer houses, more prestigious positions, and, always, more money.

We all have a need to fill our emptiness, our gaping voids, with something, anything—alcohol, opioids, shopping, gambling, sex. The stories our societies generate tell us how to fill the empty spot. But as we've seen, there is never enough. The more *stuff* we take in, the greater the hole.

It's story that got us into this situation. With kiciwamanawak, the story goes back to the religion story that facilitated agrarian society—religions that turned away from nature and toward authority. They created hierarchical social structures out of formidable stories. Those structures reinforced themselves with more stories: justice, private property, law, rights, economy, money, corporations, and most destructively, sovereignty and the modern nation-state. We have a huge web of story that perpetuates the suffering of billions to maintain the privilege of a select few.

It's all story. The constitution of Canada is a story. They wrote it. They could have written anything. It's okay, it mostly works. It's good enough. We can live with it. But we know we can also change it, rewrite it, or, more probable, reinterpret it. Stories are like that. They can change.

Here in the North, we still mostly have space to hunt, fish and gather, to find where we belong, to reconnect with our identity, to know who we are. But that's changing fast.

When my great-grandfather James Ross attended the negotiation of the adhesion to Treaty Six in 1889, it was clear that kiciwamanawak wanted to harvest the timber in this area. They also wanted the right to dig for the minerals. That's okay, we were willing to share.

Logging in this area didn't start until there was a road. In 1941, as part of the war effort, Doukhobor conscientious objectors were put to work building a highway to La Ronge. As soon as there was a road, the logging companies came. That's always been the case. The government builds the roads and infrastructure for resource extraction.

It wasn't bad at first. They only took mature trees. Logging was mostly manual labour with handsaws and axes. They skidded the logs out with horses. Sometimes our people were able to get work and even get paid. My older brothers went to the logging camps at fourteen. I didn't go until I was seventeen. I worked out there for a while before I joined the navy. In my time, it was chainsaws and mechanical skidders. In the late seventies, there were over a thousand men in the camps and a percentage of them were Indian.

It changed. They had first come for the saw logs to cut into lumber—that was in the forties. Then they came for the power poles and railroad ties in the sixties. It still wasn't too bad. They logged selectively, only taking what they could use. Then a pulp company moved in. When they came for the pulp wood in the seventies, they took everything. They clear-cut vast swathes of forest, it didn't matter the size. That's when I was in the forest along with a thousand others.

Mechanical harvesting brought an end to the big camps. With a machine, chainsaw men were not needed anymore. The camps emptied. And it still wasn't too bad. The annual allowable cut was about 1 percent of the forest. Cutting 1 percent of the forest per year allowed a hundred years for the forest to regrow. Mind you, it takes about 120 years for a tree to mature here, and for there to be very large, very old trees takes several hundred years.

Then the provincial government arbitrarily increased the annual allowable cut to 2 percent, which meant that the forest would be entirely cut within fifty years.

In 2007, Saskatchewan elected a new government who have further increased the amount the logging companies can take. The old regulations held that the companies had to leave 15 percent of the old and very old forest. It wasn't enough. They should have left at least 50 percent to ensure the survival of those species that depend upon old growth forests and to preserve the forests' integrity. Instead the government reduced the amount of old and very old forest that had to be left intact to 7 percent.

The only way to make money logging now is to cut massive amounts and earn pennies on a tree. And, of course, the government accommodates this by allocating more and more forest for cutting. The reason prices for paper and lumber have remained low is because of globalization. Countries with better climates can grow trees much faster than in cold Northern Canada. The big companies know this and have moved to places like Brazil and Indonesia. We're left with smaller companies who cannot survive without massive government subsidies. We have to pay them to cut our trees.

The reason I am telling you all of this about forestry is because it's all story. Back in the early days when the companies were being criticized over their destruction of the forest, they came up with a story. They said that their clear-cuts emulated natural disturbances, such as forest fires. The problem with the story is that there is nothing in nature that looks or behaves like a clear-cut.

When they started deforesting this territory, I began asking questions. When I asked for the science behind their regulations and decisions, I was offered conjecture. They didn't have science. They had corporate opinion. They just made stuff up. A real scientific study would compare a clear-cut area, a burned area, and an undisturbed area, then measure the amount and rate of regrowth in all three, count the species inhabiting each, and make recommendations based upon the objective results.

They didn't do that. They made up a story about how if they modified the clear-cuts so they weren't huge square blocks and had more rounded edges, and if they left the occasional tree in the middle, that their clear-cuts would look more like what happens after a fire.

After they established the story that clear-cuts look like areas burned by forest fire, they added to the story that because fire is a natural part of the landscape and sometimes pine trees regenerate quickly after a fire, that fires are good for the forest, and if fires can be seen as good for the forests, then clear-cuts, which the story says emulates fires, are also good for the forests.

We have woodland caribou here. There is a small herd of about thirty animals just across the river. They're endangered. They are the most ancient species of ungulate in North America and it's looking like their time is almost past. We know the problem is habitat loss. We know that logging is destroying habitat. The federal government mandated the provinces to come up with a plan to save the caribou. This province's plan was bizarre. They didn't do any studies, they didn't use science. They made up a story instead.

Before all the logging, the caribou were everywhere. We know the caribou stay in those areas where logging has not occurred. That is, in mostly muskeg areas that are too expensive to log and have little or no marketable timber. The province called those areas, where the caribou remain, tier one. Tier two areas were those areas adjacent to tier one areas, where we occasionally see caribou. Tier three areas are those areas so damaged by logging and concomitant habitat destruction that caribou no longer go there.

The province's plan to save the caribou is to make massive clear-cuts in those areas they designated as tier two. They are cutting as much wood as they can, as close to where the caribou are, as is economical.

They are not leaving the old and very old growth areas that caribou prefer. They are taking everything they can get their hands on.

The story they came up with to go along with the devastation is that once that area is cut over, they will withdraw and leave it for the caribou, and in about forty years the trees will have grown back. Problem is, forty-year-old forests are too young for caribou. Caribou are not found in areas that were harvested even sixty years ago. That—and the caribou probably don't have forty years to wait.

But it's a good story.

The other story the province and the logging companies tell is about economics. They provide huge numbers asserting that logging is profitable. But when you look closely at those numbers, they're filled with multipliers. They assume that for every job in a sawmill there are three associated waitress jobs in town. They have added in all the assumed spinoff economics. Of course, the story isn't true. The reason the big pulp companies left this province is because they knew they had overharvested the forests and there wasn't enough money to be made here.

The only way the present operators are surviving is through government subsidies. They pay next to nothing for royalties. The government accommodates the industry by reducing regulations that preserve the forest. They change the story. They make up new ones.

Here we are, caught in these stories—impoverished, often suicidal, trapped in despair and hopelessness, often self-medicating trauma with substance use.

Two stories.

One—the forest is a place of healing where we as Aboriginal Peoples can reconnect with our identities and our sense of belonging.

Two—the forest provides economic grounds to further political objectives.

Economics is a powerful story. It permeates all of modern thought. It overshadows even the powerful religions of the world. Christianity, Islam, Judaism, Buddhism, Hinduism have all become economic actors. These powerful stories have been subsumed into the economics story and because of it, we have all become poorer. If we don't tell our story in line with the economics story, we are not listened to. It has become the overarching genre of storytelling.

So, I, too, will tell this story in economic terms.

Imagine, if you will, a thousand Camp Hopes, places where people of the world can come and heal. From places like New York and Delhi and London and Singapore. We will preserve as much of the forest as remains in its pristine form, and people who are overstressed from being driven to their deaths by economics can come and reconnect with their authentic selves. Remember for many of them it has been over ten thousand years since they were hunter-gatherers and were connected with nature. We'll charge them a modest fee to attend these healing centres. We'll employ those of us who remember how to live on and with the land to act as guides for those who have forgotten their connections.

We know the climate is changing. We know that pristine forests will become the last refuge of humanity. Our boreal forest, this powerful, dynamic living story, can soothe our own damaged stories, reconnect the lines, overwrite the damage, and reshape us into authentic, connected, beautiful beings again.

The reason there is so much opposition to Aboriginal Peoples' rights to hunting, fishing, trapping, and gathering is because our settler relatives, kiciwamanawak, do not know the story of treaty. In their story, they came here as pioneers, broke the land, and through their own hard work and perseverance built a great nation. In that story, we are encumbrances, we stand in the way.

Our story of treaty is different. In our story, treaty making was an adoption ceremony. Remember, we were hunter-gatherers. We understood that we were related to everything. Not just familial relationships, aunts, uncles, cousins, we knew we were related to our brothers the animals and the trees. We understood the fish to live in their nation and the birds in theirs. We knew our ancestors' atoms were in the plants and animals we were related to. We knew we were related to the spirit world and called Kicimanito, the Great Spirit, our grandfather.

So, two stories.

In one, an incoming people assume control over the original people and take control over the territory, allowing the original inhabitants certain rights. In the other story, a new people arrive and are adopted by the original people, thereby giving the new people the right to coexist in the territory.

Tonight, we have Aboriginal and non-Aboriginal people sitting around here. We need to find a story that we can share, like we share the heat from this fire. We need to learn to live like family.

Woodland Cree is the name that was put on us. We call ourselves Nehithaw, which means *the people*. The name *Cree* is a slur. It refers to how easily we were Christianized. Nehithaw, the people, never had full-time chiefs. Other nations did. Our relatives the Plains Cree had full-time chiefs. The nations out on the West Coast had hereditary chiefs and maybe even kings and queens. But we didn't. We had Okemaw. When another people moved into our territory and we needed this territory to survive, we asked our best warrior to be Okemaw, or leader. When the conflict was over, when we forced the invaders out or we were forced to move, we had to let that Okemaw become one of the people again, because it's not right to put someone outside of the people.

We did the same thing with hunting. We would ask our best hunter to be Okemaw for the hunt, and, again, when it was over, when we were having a feast after the hunt, we had to let the Okemaw become one of the people again.

That didn't change until recently. I remember being a kid here. I was only about six or seven years old, and I was out with my cousins. Usually, we had to listen to whoever was the oldest, and that day it would have been Doreen. This thing about the oldest kid in a bunch being responsible was pretty ingrained. If a kid got hurt and started crying, an adult would first ask who was the oldest there, and that kid would get in trouble because they were supposed to be looking out for the younger children.

That day we were going on an adventure, and Doreen told us younger kids we had to listen to Johnny because he knew the most about hunting and being out in the bush. He was going to be our Okemaw. We went on a long hike, miles away from the community. The older kids looked after me, and we all did what Johnny instructed.

This is completely different than the democracy story.

Remember that kiciwamanawak only evolved from monarchy to democracy after they encountered free people in the Americas. They weren't able to imagine their own freedom until they experienced our example. When it comes to degrees of democracy, our system was the most liberal, some might say the most anarchical. We only had government that was absolutely necessary, and no more. We had developed the highest degree of democracy: true rule by the people, people who understood they were in charge of their lives, but when stories of governance collide, we are portrayed as simplistic and childlike.

Imagine a workplace where the workers ask one of their number to be Okemaw until a task is done. The person recognized as the best road builder would lead construction, the best firefighter would organize the firefighters, the best at anything would be chosen by the workers to lead, and when the job was done, the chosen Okemaw would be one of the workers again, eliminating dissension or tyranny. No one would work under a terrible boss ever again, because terrible people would never be asked to be Okemaw.

If we told ourselves Okemaw stories instead of hierarchical bureaucracy stories, we might know pure democracy at every level of our society.

Some of that hot tea would be really nice about now. It's been sitting by the fire all this time, so it should be nice and strong. I like it that way. But more importantly, it will be hot. It's sure starting to cool off out here, isn't it.

Governance before the Indian Act?

That's easy.

We were governed by stories.

Not dogma. That's the opposite. Our governance system was based on storytelling, not on story-abiding. We weren't ruled by stories.

Do you know how to visit? I mean real visiting.

It's a lost art in many places. Maybe it's because visiting is storytelling and storytelling is becoming a lost art. I know only a few who are good at visiting, and it's a pleasure to be with them. They understand story. They understand story structure and story cadence.

My great-grandmother Elizabeth Ross lived to be quite old. In her day, in this community, it had become a thing for the women, upon entering a house in the winter, to first go to the woodstove, turn around, raise their skirts, and warm their backsides. Like I said, she was old. She stumbled, fell against the stove, and gave herself a bad burn. We didn't have doctors here— the closest would have been two days by horse and wagon—and she didn't have a horse.

Blood poisoning set in, and Elizabeth knew she was going to die.

I have the story from two sources. One from my older sister Jean, who said she walked with Mom across the frozen lake to where there used to be a cabin, just down the shore about a mile from here. Jean said there were sheets hung up around the old woman's bed to give privacy, and when Mom went behind the sheets to talk to her grandmother, Jean stayed out in the main part of the cabin, closer to the door. That's it. Just a snippet from an older sister's memory, who would have only been about eight or maybe ten years old at the time, remembering her great-grandmother and how Mom had been called to come talk to the old woman on her deathbed.

Mom told me what her grandmother had to say to her. It wasn't just to her. Elizabeth had asked all her granddaughters to come see her as she lay dying. This was an old woman who had lived a much different life than you or I. She had frozen her fingers off when she was a little girl, and using only her thumbs and stubs had become accomplished at sewing and beading. Her father had taken her mother in a raid upon a camp of Ayacinawak, which directly translates to "strange Indians," our name for Blackfoot Peoples. Her mother was thirteen at the time and became her father's third wife.

When the priests came, they forced Elizabeth's father to give up two of his wives. My great-great-grandfather went into his tent and cried all night. In the morning when he came out, he had decided that he would keep his youngest wife because she needed taking care of. To his other two wives he gave each a team of horses and a wagon, and he filled both wagons with things they would need: blankets and robes and pots and axes. I don't know what the priests had to say about the staff with scalps attached to it that he kept.

Elizabeth married James Ross and travelled with him by canoe to where Prince Albert National Park is now. There they built a home and raised seven children. Those children, my grandmother's siblings, were all old by the time I came along.

Needless to say, Elizabeth had lived through a time of incredible change. She would have accompanied her husband when he attended the negotiation of the adhesion to Treaty Six. She lived through the expulsion of all the Indians from the territory that became Prince Albert National Park. They just came and told everyone, "This is a park now. You have to leave." And just like that, she lost her home—lost all the trails where she set snares, all the good fishing spots, all the places she had become accustomed to gathering berries and medicines.

Do you know what she had to tell her granddaughters? What was the most important thing she had learned in her long, eventful life?

Mom said she told them how to treat visitors. When a visitor comes to your home, you give them your best. You feed them. Even if it's your last bit of food, you give it to your guests. If they stay overnight, you give them your bed and you sleep on the floor. You give the best that you have and treat guests like they are the most important people in the world.

It's far more than what's culturally appropriate. We're not talking about a mere sociological trait here. Visiting was governance. Visiting was how we held our Nation together.

Yep, you got it. It was done primarily by the women. Men can visit too. If I've been invited to a meeting on a First Nation, I try to get there well ahead of time so that I can visit, and I find that it's during these informal visits that we resolve most of what we have come to meet about formally.

When you learn how to visit appropriately, you will understand Woodland Cree governance systems. To learn how to visit, how to be a really good visitor, you have to learn how to listen to, and tell, stories.

When I was a kid growing up here, something happened in our community that created a stir. I was too young to have been told what it was, but I was old enough to know it was something serious. The women of the community were in a flurry of visiting, walking quickly between each other's houses, serious looks on their faces. And the men—the adult men stood around with their heads down, being quiet. The flurry of visiting lasted several days, then subsided back to normal again. The men began joking with each other once more, and I never did find out what had happened or what the visiting had been about.

It wasn't gossip. Visiting is storytelling. But it's not gossip. We have very strong admonitions against gossip in our culture. We know that stories are powerful and negative stories can kill. All the traditional teachers I have encountered in my life, all the knowledge keepers, every one has warned against gossip and taught how it was not acceptable in our original ways of being. We are not only told to not gossip, we are told to not allow gossip into our homes.

We know today that online bullying, a modern form of gossip, has resulted in suicides. We shouldn't be surprised. We knew this. We knew that gossip could kill, that words were warfare. We knew the dangers. We just stopped reminding each other of the power of stories as we became enmeshed in this modern world and forgot the teachings available from Elders and knowledge keepers.

I have been privileged to have met some very accomplished visitors, people who remembered how it was done. When my older brother lay dying, and we were sitting with him in his final hours as he taught us how to die, my mother's cousin Nancy sat beside me and visited. She told me and my brother gentle little stories. Stories of no consequence, nothing important or even memorable. Just slightly funny little stories that helped us through those hard hours.

Later, I realized what she had done.

Nancy would have been one of my great-grandmother's granddaughters, who had been called to hear the old woman's last words. Nancy would have sat with people as they died. She knew how to be a visitor. We've mostly lost that today. Most of our people die in hospitals now, and we have lost the knowledge of how to die, how to be with the family, how to visit and the power of stories. In her quiet, gentle way, Nancy visited with us, shared her peaceful little stories, and with her voice she eased my brother's passing. I can think of no better way to leave this world than to be accompanied by a gifted visitor.

Yeah, you're getting it. A storyteller to tell the way out.

It's all there in the stories.

Everything you need to know about yourself, your history, your connection to this place, to this time, is all contained in the story that you author for yourself.

If you tell a story, it will manifest itself. Your sense of reality, what you see, comes from the stories you tell yourself. This plane of existence we experience and call life is a web of interwoven stories. We become the stories we tell ourselves.

So, there it is.

Your story. You get to author it any way you want.

It's your story, your journey. You are good storytellers, you can take the plot from here forward and create your masterpiece.

You're still here.

I thought I was done.

I will try to sum it all up as best I can. Why is the world in the shape it's in right now? What we're seeing is a whole bunch of people who don't give a shit because of the story they are telling themselves. The dominant story right now, the one we need to change, is about the primacy of the individual and their personal rights.

I saw a post on Facebook the other day. Yes, I am going to look at my phone. Just give me a second.

Here it is. Someone posted this.

YOU KNOW FOLKS, I never cared that you were
gay until you started shoving it down my throat
and I never cared what colour you were until
you started blaming me for your problems, and I
never cared about your political affiliations until
you started condemning me for mine. I really
never even cared where you were born until
you wanted to erase my history, and blame my
ancestors for your problems, you know I never
even cared that your beliefs were different than
mine, until you said my beliefs were wrong, but
now I care, my patience and tolerance are gone,
and I am not alone in feeling like this, there are
millions of us who feel like this.

Now I'll put my phone back away.

This guy doesn't care that LGBTQ people are being
killed. He doesn't care that police are murdering Black
people. He doesn't care about the planet or that the
climate is changing. He doesn't care that Aboriginal
people don't have clean water. He doesn't care that our
women are being murdered and are disappearing. He
doesn't care that our children are committing suicide.
The information age has started showing him that
there are many stories outside of the one he knows,
but he simply does not know how to give a shit. He
might not even know how to care about himself.

I saw something else the other day that also stuck in my head. It was a chart. It showed the increased deaths among subpopulations within the United States since the turn of the twenty-first century. Four lines on this graph: white people with a college degree, white people without a college degree, Black people with a college degree, and Black people without a college degree. All of these populations experienced an increase in mortality to varying degrees. White people without a college degree were the most severely impacted, followed by Black people without a college degree, and Black people with a college degree fared better than white people with a college degree.

The article said that these increased deaths were due to despair. That people were dying from alcoholism, opiate overdoses, and suicide. The increases in these deaths between the late 1990s and the first decades of the twenty-first century were so severe that they brought down the life expectancy of people living in the United States by more than two years.

Imagine waking up in the morning dreading the coming day. Imagine dreading life. We can't expect these people to give a shit about others. They're too wrapped up in their own misery. They have feelings, they feel the pain of their existence, and that pain is so strong that they cannot feel empathy for the suffering of others. They need alcohol to get through their day. They need opiates to dull the pain of their being, and when these don't work, they resort to their guns for relief.

So, we have a large segment of the population who are in pain and cannot give a shit about the others in that population who are hurting. And the people who are hurting are hurting because so many others don't give a shit. If we all cared, we could end racism, we could do something about climate change and the future for our children. Caring is a powerful place-bo. If you tell someone you care about them, you can change their life.

I was told a story by one of our women. She was a sex worker on the street. It was a horrible day for her, one of her darkest. She was standing there, waiting for a trick, hoping it wouldn't be a bad one, when a wom-an and her husband walked by. They walked on a lit-tle way, and then the woman turned around and came back. She didn't say anything, just gave our friend a hug. That's it. No words. Just a hug. Showed that she gave a shit.

It changed our friend's life. She left the street that day, got herself clean, and is now working to help oth-er women get off the street.

Giving a shit is a powerful story.

A common difference between people who live well into their hundreds and people who don't is that people who are cared about often live longer. Sometimes it's that simple. If you are in a story where you feel warm and welcome and wanted, you will stay in that story longer. If you're not wanted, if you become an ancillary character in your own story, you may stop wanting to be here.

We know this. This isn't anything new. Mind, body, emotion, and spirit are all connected. The stories we tell ourselves can heal us or kill us. So we see in the United States, and Canada is never far behind what happens there, that the story of that nation is now killing the people. The story promised them success and wealth and prosperity. It said if you come here, or are born here, in the promised land, and if you work hard, you, too, can have all you ever wanted. You can be a somebody. Then there were a whole bunch of people that the story failed to deliver for. The story told them that because they didn't have a fancy car, a big house, four televisions, and a stock market portfolio that they were failures, that they were losers.

Now you have to imagine how powerful this story is, this Western democracy story, this capitalist story. We are so bombarded with it that it is in everything we see and hear. This is the story of the marketplace, of the economy, of Wall Street, of banks, of big tech, and big pharma. It's a story retold in every advertisement that promises if you buy this product your life will be better. During COVID, we have accepted that people have to die so that businesses don't suffer. It's a powerful story. It's so complete that most people accept it as natural, normal, and necessary.

And when it fails, when the story doesn't give what it promised—then people suffer. The more they suffer, the less they care about each other—the less they give a shit, the more others suffer. The reason might be because of the story we made up, but the suffering is real. What we're all experiencing, white people, Black people, LGBTQ people, Aboriginal people, is real suffering.

The best way to alleviate that suffering is to create a new story, an inclusive story where no one is left out. When people see themselves as part of a shared story, they can relate to the other characters in that story. When we start to tell this new story, and people begin to feel like they belong in it, then they will start to give a shit about each other. We all need to be in a story that tells us that we are wanted, that we are cared for, and that we belong.

But that's enough for tonight.

Okay, one more.

But, just one.

Kayas,

Well, I guess not *kayas* in the way it is normally meant. Usually, kayas means *long time ago*. It is the first word in every traditional story. Here I am using it more in the sense of "once upon a time"—in story-time—yes, stories have their own time—past, present, and future, as Einstein said, is nothing more than a persistent illusion.

So,

Kayas, Wisahkicahk had forgot many of the teachings of the Creator. He still remembered a few things, not much, enough to get by.

At that time the scientists were working on solving the problem of reality. They knew that most of physical reality was empty space, that the atoms that made up physical things were very tiny, and they really didn't know what kept everything together. What was this mystical glue?

One scientist in particular was very determined. He wanted to be the first to solve the mystery. The harder he worked, the more frustrated he became. With frustration came anger. His anger drove him harder and harder until, finally, he succeeded in breaking the bond between atoms. It sounded like cloth being torn, and from somewhere he heard someone say "ouch." He had put a hole in reality itself.

The scientist became very worried because the hole he had created began to grow. Like a hole in anything will get larger by itself, so, too, did the hole that the scientist had put in reality. There was no way of stopping the hole from getting larger. It looked like a black ball that kept growing. Anything that went into the hole disappeared because its atoms were no longer held together. Since all things are made of atoms that are far apart, when the force that holds them together is destroyed, the atoms, being very small, have no strength.

The scientist tried putting lead around the black ball. Lead is a very dense material. It slowed the hole from growing a little, but since the hole was created by destroying the force that held atoms together, even lead, which is made from atoms, could not do more than slow the hole from growing.

Strange things began to happen.

Animals were attracted to the hole. Like a moth to a flame, so, too, were all the animals attracted to the hole. Insects buzzed at the window to the laboratory and crawled under the door. Birds tried flying into the building. Animals from the forest came into the city to be near the hole. Any animal that was able to get into the hole did—and disappeared because its atoms were no longer held together.

The people found out what was going on because the scientists could not keep it a secret with all the animals on the Earth acting strange and trying to get into the laboratory. The people were afraid when they found out. Existence was in danger, and the scientists could not save it. Some scientists said that the hole could be used to get rid of nuclear waste, which they had a lot of in those days, but the people would not let them. The people no longer trusted the scientists, and besides, no one knew for certain what would happen if nuclear waste was put into the hole.

Something had to be done. The animals would not stay away from the hole. All day, eagles soared over the laboratory waiting for a chance to get to the hole. Lions tried to get out of zoos, which was the only place left where they existed. A herd of elephants drowned trying to swim across the ocean. Whales threw themselves up on the shore. So did fishes and turtles. The people were afraid that if they did not do something that there would be no animals left on the Earth. The people were especially afraid because bears and wolves were walking into the city and the people were afraid to go outdoors. They decided that they would send the hole far out into outer space. Perhaps even to the end of the universe.

Wisahkicahk asked if he could steer the spaceship that took the hole far away. He told the scientists that he would steer the spaceship for as long as he was alive, because it would take longer than many lifetimes to get to there, then he would point the spaceship toward the end of the universe before he died. The scientists agreed to let him go because it was important that nothing happen to the spaceship that carried the dangerous hole until it was very far from the Earth. If the hole was free to grow, it would swallow up the Earth, the moon, the other planets, and even the sun.

Wisahkicahk was alone in the spaceship far from the Earth. He had brought a Sacred Pipe along on the trip to pray with. He prayed very hard. He had given his life for Creation and would die alone among the stars to take the hole far away from the people he loved. He was a little afraid of dying, and he was very lonely. He prayed with such sincerity that a spirit from the other side in the shape of an eagle came to Wisahkicahk in the spaceship. Wisahkicahk was grateful for the company and began to talk to the eagle spirit.

He said, "Spirit, you must be able to travel very fast and must know how far it is to the end of the universe. Can you take this hole to the end of the universe for me so that I can go back home?"

The eagle spirit answered that the end of the universe was not very far away. In fact, the end of the universe was the hole that Wisahkicahk was trying to take there. Then the spirit left. Wisahkicahk was confused. How could he take the hole that was the end of the universe to the end of the universe?

Again, Wisahkicahk brought out his pipe and prayed. The spirit returned, this time as a bear. Wisahkicahk told the bear spirit that he could not figure out how to take the hole that was the end of the universe to the end of the universe and asked the bear spirit to help him get rid of the hole. The bear spirit said he could not. Man had made the hole in existence, and man would have to mend the hole. Then the bear spirit left.

Once more, Wisahkicahk filled his pipe and prayed. This time when the spirit returned, it came as a woman. Wisahkicahk was surprised. He was about to say something when the woman said, "Humans are sacred animals, too, Wisahkicahk."

Wisahkicahk thought about that for a moment. Yes, it was true. Humans were sacred animals, too, but most had forgotten. He asked the human spirit how men could mend the hole they had put in existence.

The spirit answered, "Do like the animals that love existence so much they are willing to give their lives to mend it."

After the spirit left, Wisahkicahk was alone in the spaceship. He thought about going into the hole if that would repair it. He would give his life that the hole would be healed. But Wisahkicahk had to be sure that if he gave his life to the hole that it would be mended. So, for the fourth time he filled his pipe and prayed, and for the fourth time a spirit came to him. This time in the form of a wolf.

Wisahkicahk asked the wolf spirit why would the hole be mended if he went into it. Did the hole demand a human sacrifice?

The wolf spirit laughed at Wisahkicahk. He said, "You humans believe that you are the most important of all Creation because you are the most destructive. The animals that tried to give their lives to the hole did so because they loved existence. They came to the hole to give their love. They loved so much that they were willing to give their lives."

Now Wisahkicahk was very confused. He asked the wolf spirit how it was that an emotion such as love could mend a hole in existence. How was it that when the force that kept the atoms together was broken, love could mend it?

The wolf spirit explained that existence was love. The force that kept the atoms together was the Great Spirit, and the Great Spirit was love. It was only because the scientist was very, very angry that he was able to put a hole in the Great Spirit. It was the Great Spirit who had said "ouch" when the scientist put a little hole in him.

So, Wisahkicahk filled his heart with love for all of existence, which is the Creator, and the hole slowly closed itself back up. Then Wisahkicahk turned the spaceship around and came back to the Earth. That is how we know to love all of Creation, and why we try so hard to live in harmony with the animals and plants that are our relatives in Creation. We are all held together by the same force that keeps our atoms from drifting apart. It is a love story.

Now we are done. It's starting to get dark, and some of you still have to take a boat back across the lake to where you parked your vehicles. It's been great to sit around this fire with you, to experience each of you as unique, special human beings. Thank you for coming to visit me. Thank you for taking time out of your lives to come here. Thank you for your attention.

Hiy hiy, kakithaw nawakomakanak. All my relations.

HAROLD R. JOHNSON (1954–2022) was the author of six works of fiction and six works of nonfiction, including *Firewater: How Alcohol is Killing My People (and Yours)*, which was a finalist for the Governor General's Literary Award for Nonfiction. Born and raised in northern Saskatchewan to a Swedish father and a Cree mother, Johnson served in the Canadian Navy and worked as a miner, logger, mechanic, trapper, fisherman, tree planter, and heavy-equipment operator. He graduated from Harvard Law School and managed a private practice for several years before becoming a Crown prosecutor. He was a member of the Montreal Lake Cree Nation.

Printed in the USA
CPSIA information can be obtained
at www.ICGtesting.com
JSHW020949291223
R13210800005B/R132108PG54313JSX00016B/11